VG

SPEARFISH

BRIAN CALLISON

◆

SPEARFISH

COLLINS
8 Grafton Street, London
1983

William Collins Sons and Co. Ltd.
London · Glasgow · Sydney · Auckland
Toronto · Johannesburg

British Library Cataloguing in Publication Data

Callison, Brian
  Spearfish.
  I. Title
  823'.914[F]   PR6053.A39
  ISBN 0-00-222684-7

Photoset in Linotron Sabon
by Rowland Phototypesetting Ltd
Bury St Edmunds, Suffolk
Made and Printed in Great Britain by
William Collins Sons and Co. Ltd, Glasgow

CHAPTER ONE

Troop Sergeant Bosche scrabbled dazedly in his own blood, claw-frantic hands exploring fearfully towards belly, crotch – his curiously foreshortened legs . . . and only then did his eyes slam wide open, appalled and staring from red-rimmed pits of shock as realisation hit him.

Already Crofts could hear the Angolan irregulars nervously moving in; the crackle of Column Delta's blazing trucks, the gentle sizzle of cordite-fuelled cremation – the clipped cautions of Cuban advisers as the first mercenary corpses were bayoneted or gutted with razor-edged pangas. Just to make bloody certain.

Bosche must have sensed them coming too. Abruptly he began pleading; animal-whimpering with gory hands now tendered in shuddering appeal. The mutilated man's words were indistinguishable – though Crofts wouldn't have understood them even had they been spoken clearly from a throat unconstricted by the horror of what had just happened to Sergeant Bosche. Amid the frenetic panic of ambush a German dies in German, a Frenchman dies in French, a British soldier dies in a welter of Anglo-Saxon epithets when he loses all hope. But Crofts already knew what was required of him . . . positively *demanded* of him by the rules of the killing game they had both entered as fully-aware professionals.

The butt of the heavy calibre Beretta felt cold against his palm as he raised it towards Bosche's dust-caked forehead. The expression in the German's eyes was softening perceptibly; glazing from his earlier terror to an enormous brother-loving gratitude – only something was terribly wrong, all of a sudden! Croft's own right hand was glistening red now, his revulsion-stiff forefinger fumbling tiredly to enter the trigger guard. There was blood coming from him *too*, f'r God's sake! Flowing steadily from his arm; thinner, more watery than he'd ever remembered from previous wounds but it was his, nevertheless. As the pain locked on he began to fade; nausea swamping him in gagging, sweating waves. He couldn't pull the trigger; couldn't live up to his promise of years before to pre-empt what was about to happen to Troop Sergeant Bosche when the hunters discovered he was still alive. Please! Please let me squeeze that trigger, Lord? PLEASE show the mercy to let me blow the top of Hermann Bosche's bloodied skull away . . .

. . . beside him the girl sighed, raised herself on one elbow and blinked uncertainly down at Crofts through a cascade of long blonde hair.

'Did you ask for something?'

Crofts' eyes were open too, now. Like Sergeant Bosche's had been, every time he shrieked through that recurring nightmare. Only in the Sergeant's case there hadn't been a beautiful body to stare at: simply a nine-millimetre void in the muzzle of a Beretta M951. While even that remained mute, extending a milli-second of ultimate fear into an eternity of anticipation, sadistically refusing to detonate one last violent kindness . . .

'No,' Crofts said quietly. 'I've learned never to ask for things any more.'

The girl was silent for a moment, then she wriggled until she was above and astride him, the sheet slipping unconcernedly from her arched back. Poised against a backdrop of early morning light filtering through the hotel curtains she appeared provocatively ethereal; exquisite shoulders a wax-pale consequence of the waning London winter, the texture of her skin flawless as only nineteen, maybe twenty years of youth could hope to retain.

Tenderly lifting Crofts' hand from the pillow she lowered her head, parting her lips to envelope his thumb, then gnawing gently, her eyes never leaving his. Oh, there was such contrast there, such an ingenuous depravity; a sweetness of innocence, yet at the same time a comprehensivity of carnal wisdom. Unmoving he returned her gaze, while reflecting with consciously cynical prurience upon the multiform intimacies revealed by the animal child through the course of that night; her so flagrantly exhibited and faintly arrogant beauty humanised – and thereby made immeasurably more sensual – by the uncontrolled spasms of harlot ugliness betrayed during their peaks of total abandonment.

A great many peaks. Ego-boosting peaks for him; and so desperately needed.

'I've never been to bed with anyone as old as you before,' she said softly. But there was no contempt. It was simply a statement; a wide-eyed appreciation. A happy realisation.

He frowned gravely. 'Hardly surprising really; there aren't that many of us left. I'm forty-seven, you know. Virtually over the hill as a useful human being.'

She took his hand again until he felt her jaw tense, her teeth sharp and trembling around the base of his thumb; fighting the temptation to begin again. He didn't, dammit he couldn't respond . . . eventually, grudgingly, she raised her head and laid the underside of his wrist along her cheek, smothering it delightfully under waterfalling strands. Idly he noticed the tropical burn of his arm against the arched milk throat, simultaneously registering the fragmentation scar carved by the Soviet-manufactured anti-tank mine, still obscene as a violent purple slash from shoulder to elbow; his personal legacy from the mercenary trade. Contrast yet again! Maiden skin; sun-ravaged hide. Flawless body; battle-savaged frame. The insatiable libido of youth – with only the edge-blunting defence of maturity to maintain his own failing search for completeness.

Yet was his need truly that of mere sexual fulfilment? Or was it more complex than he cared to admit; more a need *for* a need? To prove to himself that he wasn't really growing old; that his desires of the moment were every bit as driving as the ruttish ambitions experienced by Captain Michael Crofts of the Parachute Regiment some twenty years ago – before the mercenary recruiters bought him, and

7

his ideals dissolved in other men's blood paid for by the gallon!

'You're very good at making love,' she whispered. And Crofts felt happy for the first time since Troop Sergeant Bosche had died, because that was precisely what he wanted – needed – to hear.

She bowed her head and the hair splayed across his chest with silken delicacy. He became aware of her lips brushing the scar on his arm, her tongue flicking it with lascivious curiosity, and he guessed she was challenging him to explain. But he didn't. Because you can't expect a child to understand the sick horror of a betrayed campaign; to visualise the straggle of flaring, eviscerated personnel carriers and the merciless yammer of the concealed R.P.D.'s and the grue of human offal and terror-excrement and severed limbs fouling the ambush ground. Certainly not the vision of heads without torsos which smile inanely up at you from the bullet-exploding dust yet still affording a drained, grisly familiarity with comrades-in-arms who'd faced you across the mess table only that morning . . .

While how could you possibly describe the shrieks of a twenty-year-long friend called Hermann Bosche, who'd shuffled all of thirty metres towards the fragile cover of the jungle on bloodied stumps before he discovered his lower legs and manhood had been blown away in the first moments of the attack – and only then had keeled over and prayed for Crofts to shoot before the Marxist black men finally caught up with him.

Crofts *had* contrived to murder Troop Sergeant Bosche out of love, in the end. But it was odd, really – that he'd never actually managed to pull that trigger again. Not once, throughout all the constantly-recurring nightmares.

The telephone rang. A smoothly professional woman's voice announced, 'Seven-thirty, sir. Breakfast is being served in the Carvery Restaurant. Good morning!'

Crofts said 'Thank you,' then lay back and fumbled for a cigarette. Even after three months he still found it an indulgence to awake to the smell of femininity and the plastic politeness of five star living, rather than the rotting stink of Namibia or Cambodia or the Yemen accompanied by the hoarse disenchantment of sleep-starved men in camouflaged fatigues. Yet he was also uneasily aware that luxury, as a matter of course, becomes a jaded mode; that already he was restless with the aimless life despite his previous determination to retire.

The girl hesitated, watching him a moment longer, then slipped out of bed just a little petulantly. He inhaled gratefully, eyeing her through the writhing blue-grey smoke as she stretched, the now so-enchantingly-vandalised silk slipping from her shoulders in a tumble of golden highlights. There was no brazen intent prompting the statuesque nudity; simply a hedonistic awareness of her own perfection.

'You're very good as well,' he said, awkwardly conscious of the understatement. 'Thank you!'

He was surprised and pleased when she smiled gratefully, even shyly for the first time, and he suddenly wondered whether she, too, had suffered the fears of inadequacy. Perhaps the difference in their ages had presented as formidable a challenge to her as it had to him – only in the girl's case the uncertainty, with exquisite irony, had been that her youthfulness might have proved deficient against his worldly experience.

'Can I use your toothbrush?' she asked; then looked a little doubtful. 'Or perhaps you'd rather I didn't? It's not very hygienic.'

Crofts reflected on the mutual excesses of their love play during the preceding hours and tried hard not to smile; to appear a serious debater.

'If you don't mind, then I don't. It's with my shaving kit in the bathroom. You can even shower with my soap if you want to.'

She bent and kissed him on the tip of his nose. 'You really are nice. Can I see you again?'

'Only if you promise not to use all the soap.'

Her eyes were wide and blue and suddenly hurt. 'Now you're making fun of me.'

'Honestly, I'd love to see you again. Often . . .' He glanced at his watch; it was twenty-to-eight. 'Didn't you say you were meeting someone this morning?'

She shrugged. 'Only Daddy. Ten o'clock in Harvey Nichols' basement coffee shop. He's driving into town for the day.'

'Better not be late then. He'll be irritable enough already after hunting for a parking space in Knightsbridge.'

'Graham will find one. He always does.'

'Graham? Is he your brother, then? Or a friend?'

She looked matter-of-fact. 'He's Daddy's chauffeur, of course.'

'Of course,' Crofts murmured, and thought uncomfortably again of the previous night; the manner in which they'd met. He'd bumped into her in the hotel lift while still undecided on how to spend yet another lonely evening in the loneliest city in the world, then had found himself drawn into conversation so easily that he'd been cynical of her true motive; initially suspicious that her unconcealed interest was merely a subtle prelude to sexual commercialism. But if her room on the next floor was already bought and paid for, while now it also appeared that Daddy had a chauffeur . . .?

'It sounds as though, next time,' he said, unintentionally sarcastic, 'you'll even be able to afford your own soap.'

The girl stared at him for a moment, tracing the scar on his arm thoughtfully; ever so gently. 'You thought I was a prostitute at first, didn't you?' she challenged without the slightest trace of embarrassment.

He eyed her, wondering if his guilt was too apparent.

'For a little while. Right at the beginning,' he temporised cautiously.

'And . . . would you have hired me if I had been?'

He smiled. 'Being more than wise after the event – yes.'

'For, say, fifty pounds?'

Crofts frowned, struggling to keep it jocular. 'Probably. That's about all I had on me – unless you were prepared to take American Express?'

Abruptly she held out her hand, watching his reaction with an alien excitement he'd never seen before. Her skin was flushed now yet, in the same moment, harlot-cold.

'The fifty will do, please. For the screw!'

For a long time Crofts gazed at her, his expression tight, but his inner self absorbing the greatest hurt – the psychological need so euphorically fulfilled only to be cruelly replaced by self-contempt for his own Judas vanity. He found himself slowly reaching for his wallet and counting five ten-pound notes into her outstretched palm. Bitterly he considered deducting a derisory sum in advance for the use of the toothbrush, but he didn't; there was no humour in him any more. No happy feeling.

Her head bent as she fingered the money, caressing it; displaying a seemingly excessive satisfaction with her gain. At first he watched with sick anger, repelled yet hypnotised by the quickening swell of her breasts, the strangely excited pulse throbbing in the still-tantalisingly graceful curve of her neck. Oh, he could have refused, sure. He could take it from her now. He could abuse her physically, savagely; even end her if he wanted to – he'd already killed for money many times, though always impersonally before. Men, women, barely-formed children inevitably died in the scrofulous little wars followed by mercenary soldiers such as Crofts.

But he didn't. Because despite her slut-insensitive sophistication she was still too beautiful, too fragile for him to hate half as much as he now hated himself. So he simply turned his face unseeingly towards the wall, at least denying her the enjoyment of his humiliation. And felt very tired, even more lonely than before.

Distantly he sensed her rise from the bed, heard the rustle of the notes as she stood over him . . . then her voice. Only this time it was as soft as before, with only the faintest trace of censure.

'You hurt me, you know. Laughing at me like that. But maybe I'm secretly glad. You see, until now I've always lacked the courage to indulge in a very personal fantasy . . .'

He rolled over, confused. Neatly she was replacing the notes in his wallet; returning it to the bedside table. Then she bent and kissed him impishly.

'I've always wanted to be a real whore. Even for a little while.'

For a long moment he lay blinking at the outrageous

woman-child who had first undermined, then so mischievously reprieved his wavering egotism. And savoured the return of warmth to his loins.

Only then did Crofts take her willing hand and draw her down beside him.

'If it helps then – at least technically – I'm sure you'll qualify as one forever,' he pronounced gravely, 'from the moment you accept the use of *my* bloody soap!'

CHAPTER TWO

Crofts relaxed, listening to the sounds from the girl in the shower; staring round the darkened room and thinking. Every so often his gaze would rest on the multi-labelled suitcase on the rack, and a flicker of uncertainty would stir. Eventually he lit another Lucky Strike and slipped out of bed, moving towards the bulk of his worldly possessions. Crossing the room he caught his reflection in the mirror and hesitated, diverted; frowning at the image and feeling slightly ridiculous as he tried to visualise International Man Crofts seen through the girl's eyes – the havoc that time and physical abuse could wreak on the human frame.

Though was he really so unattractive? Oh, sure, the consequences of violence were brutally apparent. His most recent ambush scar. The tissue-white indent in the right thigh, impacted when an Egyptian bullet had slammed him against the mud wall of a Yemeni O.P. over a decade ago. The never-quite-faded pitting across his chest from the point blank detonation of that antiquated shotgun – which would have been lethal instead of merely terrifying if it hadn't exploded most of its home-made charge into the Terr's face as he pulled the trigger, thereby preventing yet another ZAPU freedom fighter from hailing the dawn of the new Zimbabwe. And, of course, Crofts' first battle wound of all – recalling the excruciating rake of razor-sharp ceremonial steel lion's claws across his back; earned through fear out of inexperience, before the fanatical Congolese Simba rebel withered under a full Sten magazine emptied into him by an equally young and terrified Eric Harley all those years ago.

But still . . . he drew himself erect and smirked at the idiot reflection prancing naked before him. Tall – yeah! Well built? He allowed himself to shrug a suitably modest affirmative. Physically fit? Well, he was still breathing, wasn't he? With most of his parts still in place and functioning. So how about looks then? Crofts facile self-satisfaction gradually converted to a ferocious glower while he experimented with 'handsome', conceded as far as 'rugged', then retreated even further down the scale to 'interestingly masculine'.

As what was left of his vanity crumbled he growled 'Shit!' at his double, then caught sight of the suitcase again. Frowning, he lifted the lid and probed under the neatly layered shirts, taking out the gun. It still felt cold. Almost as cold as it had done on the day he used it to blow poor bloody Hermann away.

Depressing the release he withdrew the eight-round clip from the ridged alloy grip with unsettlingly familiar ease, the brass cases of 9 mm Parabellums glinting evilly within their oiled box magazine. Sharply he pulled the slide to the rear, the gun held away from him and slightly to one side. Leaving the hammer cocked above the empty chamber he gazed down at the gun expressionlessly. It was unloaded now for the first time since he'd discharged himself from the trade. His first gesture towards normalisation; towards dropping his guard.

But it was hard to side-step the shadows of the past. You didn't simply retire from Crofts' profession; just hang up your grenades and fade into quiet obscurity. Crofts had been an irritating if minor thorn in many a Third World power-seeker's hide for too many years. The outrage of the political extremist or the religious fanatic simmers long and hard; there were several now in positions of supremacy who would cheerfully order his termination should he carelessly present himself as a target of opportunity – yet on the other hand he had to begin his reintegration into peaceful society somewhere; take a first step in the hope that his new world might be one of normalcy, where violence existed merely as a remote headline or an impersonal image on a television screen.

Certainly Crofts felt more at ease that morning than he'd

ever done since he'd returned; much more willing to make his first gesture towards settlement. Maybe it was the result of the healing period through which he'd passed – the quiet, anonymous time when brutality was only present in his nightmares and battle a tight-lipped memory – but he liked to think it was more meaningful than that; to credit his new contentment to the girl. The way she had persuaded him to smile without strain, to relax. Had reminded him of a too-long-denied sensation called 'tenderness'.

Deliberately he balanced the weapon across the palm of his hand and gazed at it, willing himself to remember. It took very little effort; immediately he could smell the burning corpses and the sick-sweet drift of cordite and, more particularly, the tangible stench of Troop Sergeant Bosche's horror-sweat which had shocked him so intensely at the time, and had proved the catalyst for his own resolve to quit the mercenary game. Oh, he hadn't made his decision out of cowardice – Crofts had long accepted that personal injury and physical suffering were fellow campaigners – but the mutilation of Bosche had savagely brought home the fact that his luck had indeed time-expired. For twenty years he and Bosche, Eric Harley and Mearns had fought side by side, each believing the others were indestructible and each pinning his faith on that one tenuous conviction; always trusting in their mutual immortality to bring them through. Until Angola, Namibia and the South African connection when it all collapsed . . . when the South African High Command pulled their regulars back across the border while Mercenary Force Delta still advanced, tempted to make one last thrust so as to increase the bonus earned against their SWAPO terrorist head count. It had been at that point that the law of averages and the Angolan Army caught up; Column Delta hit the ambush, unbelievably efficiently planned even allowing for Soviet-Cuban guidance . . . and moments later Hermann Bosche had become a whimpering half-man, and Mike Crofts finally became sickened with the futility of fighting other people's wars.

He hefted the gun grimly, appreciating its familiar

balance. It wasn't nostalgia – nostalgia was for nice things; not for a part of you which dispensed only misery and anguish. But it had been a good weapon, reliable in the monsoon mud, trustworthy in the abrasive shriek of desert winds. Oh, sure, a lot of the boys had mocked it; invariably the hardeyed ones fresh from the US or the UK or the Legion, out to play the mercenary game, kill themselves a few black men an' retire on the blood money; more bucks for the bang than the regular services paid – it was always *them* who sniggered, patronised a battle-weary major holstering a 1951 Beretta which wasn't even a fully double-action automatic; never the old hands like Harley and Bosche and Harry Mearns, who'd seen what Crofts' pistol did to a man when it slammed a nine mil Parabellum into him at eleven hundred and eighty-two-feet per second.

Most of them died in Angola – the adolescent mockers: a lot of them still wearing surprised expressions at finding the black African rebel had shopped around a bit since Sanders ruled the river. For spear, read Soviet 7.62 mm AK assault rifle; for lion pit with pointed stakes, read anti-personnel mine stamped 'Made in North Korea'; for jungle drums, read AM/FM/UHF combat radio with East German microchip reliability.

Deliberately Crofts presented the Beretta at arm's length and slipped his finger inside the trigger guard, sweating now with the phantom stare of Hermann Bosche a crystal clear memory split by the blade of the foresight. It was a necessary act; a self-inflicted aversion therapy. He had to force himself to taste the sick revulsion of the recent past; to convince his wavering resolution that the future, however vulnerable he left himself, could hold no greater awfulness . . .

There was no girl now: no comfortable hotel room. Only the corpses and the yammer of the Degtyarevs cutting Column Delta into even smaller pieces, and the choked-short screams of wounded, suddenly-not-so-hard men crying for *Mutter* or *Maman* or Mother as the pangas arc-ed downwards . . . and the agonised appeal of his friend!

But he couldn't. He still couldn't squeeze the bloody TRIGGER!

Crofts felt his brain clouding; the pain exploding in his arm. Only dimly he heard the last jeep in the column; the flat-out roar of the engine as it bucketed towards him across the crumpled forms of the already and almost dead; detonating through the drifting smoke with Harley hanging back from the twin handles of the rear-mounted M2 Browning, returning the Angolan fire in controlled bursts, target selection as cool as crushed ice . . . and finally broadsiding to a halt beside him, heralding a derisive snarl from the hardest bastard of them all.

'Time to go, Major. You could say the boys just went out of business. With a bang!'

He was squinting up, trying to focus on the jeep wavering above him; windscreen shattered, grill buckled and smeared with scraps of men from the exploded truck ahead – and Mearns' cropped head leaning out, still grinning savagely; revelling as he always did in the fear and stink of action. Company Sergeant Major Mearns. Crazy Harry Mearns, flushed with the maniac euphoria of it even in defeat. Oh, sure, the CSM's eyes did grow momentarily bleak as he assessed the ragged amputations, the bloodied pelvic region, the waxen pallor of Bosche . . . the intent behind the Beretta in Crofts' hand. But there was no compassion there; not from Mearns.

'So do it, if you're goin' to. Or d'you want we should wait around till the Kraut bleeds to death in his own good time?'

Crofts felt the fury welling in him; the desire to turn the pistol on Mearns instead; blow that ruthless sneer away and so do every black man in Africa a favour. And Mearns knew it. The challenge was blatant with contempt for Crofts' weakness.

'You got another ten seconds to pull that trigger, *Mister* Crofts. Or you an' Hermann the German there – you're on your own with the chop-chop boys!'

An Angolan HMG began to feel for them through the temporary smoke screen, shells exploding monstrously across the charnel field; creeping towards Crofts like some purposeful firecracker with the puppet corpses jerking and flinging aimless arms as it vectored through. Harley's Browning racketed in reply, ejected cases clattering and falling around the men on the ground. The frantic clamour of the Degtyarev ceased abruptly.

Eric's shout now; adding to Crofts' already intolerable dilemma. An urgency to mercy . . .

'He's finished, Mike; run out of time. Dammit, man, you *owe* him!'

But in Harley's case there was a tightly contained sadness; a whole bitterness of sympathy. Warningly Mearns' foot depressed the clutch, crashing the gears. The jeep eased ahead . . . but stopped again. It was the nearest Mearns would ever get to relenting. This time his arm came over the side, cradling an M16 with one-handed casualness. It was aimed at Bosche though, and not towards the enemy.

'O.K.! So I'll do him the favour if you haven't the guts,' he surrendered almost mockingly. 'Though Christ knows, I din't even *like* the guy . . .'

Troop Sergeant Bosche began whimpering again, shaking his head from side to side and Crofts knew he didn't want it that way. Not from Mearns. Not without kindness.

A mortar shell erupted close by, slamming the jeep on its springs, showering them with foetid, smoking jungle filth but Crofts ignored it. Ever so gently he placed the muzzle of the Beretta against Bosche's forehead and took his sergeant's hand. '*Es tut mir leid, Hermann* . . .' he whispered in halting German. 'I am sorry . . .'

The snap of the hammer against the empty chamber carried the trauma of a live round exploding in the silent hotel room. For a long time Crofts stood there naked, holding the pressure on the trigger. Forcing himself to remember.

'Have you ever killed anybody with it?' the girl asked wonderingly, her voice calm and unafraid. Crofts stirred, turned. She was standing by the bathroom door with drops of water jewels against her skin, the towel clutched in her raised hand, frozen in the act of drying her hair.

'Yes,' he answered quietly. He made no attempt to hide the gun. Somehow he sensed he didn't have to.

'Many people?'

'Too many.'

She padded over and gazed at it with an uncertain frown. He could smell the soap and the toothpaste, the enchanting freshness of her now mingling with the vegetable odour of gun oil. When her eyes lifted to meet his they were wide and questioning.

'The people you killed – were they bad people?'

He shook his head slowly. 'Not really. Certainly not all of them. Some of them were just ordinary, frightened people. I'm a . . . I *was* a soldier.'

Her fingers touched his arm lightly. 'It's affected you, I could tell. But isn't it a part of being in the British Army? Having to fight for what you believe in?'

Crofts managed a faint inward smile. It was there again – the ingenuousness: her assumption that all military men were motivated by patriotism and dedication to the Queen rather than by professionalism and plain ambition. He felt a compulsion to be open with her.

'I wasn't in the British Army . . . or haven't been for many years. I just fought for regimes; would-be governments which paid the rate for the job. I didn't kill other soldiers out of patriotism, I killed them for money. And sometimes people who didn't want the wars, didn't even understand them, got caught in the cross-fire.'

Suddenly her hand stopped stroking his arm and he sensed he was in danger of losing her. 'I don't think I could feel for you if you'd ever done anything which put Daddy or myself – people in a . . . well a democracy like ours – at risk.'

He gazed at her, surprised by the intensity of feeling behind the statement and, for that matter, the inference contained in it. But he already knew how easy it was to hurt her, and how ruthless she could be in her own defence. He chose his words with great care.

'I've always fought *against* Communism; never for it, if that's what you mean. Most of the European mercenaries did have reservations in that way. Or maybe we were simply trying to justify ourselves, persuading ourselves that we were defending this democratic principle of yours because the governments who should have taken strong action backed away instead.'

'You talk in the past tense. Don't you believe it yourself any more?'

He shrugged. 'I don't think I ever did. Either way, I've retired from it. I want to grow old gracefully; not always looking over my shoulder . . . and not lose any more friends the hard way.'

She eyed him perceptively. 'You'll always be looking over your shoulder while you have that gun. This is Britain.'

'I know. I'm going to get rid of it.'

'When?'

'Today.'

She laid her fingers on his arm again. 'Why today? You've already been in London a long time.'

'I think it's because I met you,' he said simply, then hesitated. 'Did you really mean it – when you talked about feeling something for me?'

'Yes. In fact I think I could get close to you very easily.'

The happiness in him reached fever pitch but he kept it tightly controlled. He had to. Instead he glowered at her severely. 'I'm at least twice as old as you. I'm hard as nails and cynical as hell. I've lived far too long on the edge of the law and symbolise the kind of guy your family would hate on sight. Your Daddy should spank your bottom for being the irresponsible child you are!'

She smiled that deliciously unpredictable smile.

'I'd much rather *you* did the spanking! And you'd get on well with Daddy. When it comes to being cynical and hard, he can probably give you lessons.'

Putting her arms round him she laid her head against his chest. Somehow even the Beretta in his hand didn't seem cold any more, but he still pushed her firmly away.

'Anyway, I'm not entirely satisfied by all that you've told me,' he challenged. 'There's something you're keeping secret; something more I need to know about you.'

She blinked up at him through wet golden strands, openly apprehensive for the first time.

'What?'

'Your name,' he said wryly. 'I've seduced you; I've been to bed with you; I've even made an official prostitute of you . . . and I still don't know what to call you, dammit!'

She snuggled closer despite his weak protestation. 'It's Pam. Pam Trevelyan.'

'Mine's Mike. Crofts.'

'How do you do, Michael Crofts,' the girl said.

'Hello, Pamela Treveylan!'

Before he lobbed the gun towards the bed and kissed her he realised there might be a further problem on the horizon which, until then, he had found neither the courage nor the conviction to contemplate.

For it appeared that no matter how disparate their ages or how brief their knowledge of each other – they were already beginning to fall in love.

As he held the taxi door open she squeezed his hand. 'Sorry you missed breakfast.'

Crofts grinned. 'I hadn't even noticed.'

'Six o'clock, then. In the rooftop lounge?'

'It's going to seem a long day,' he affirmed gallantly, and felt a bit old fashioned. The taxi driver said, 'Where to, guv?'

'Knightsbridge. Harvey Nichols.'

Pamela frowned at the Park Lane traffic. 'Perhaps I'd be quicker walking.'

'In that snarl-up, goin' to *Australia* you'd be quicker walking,' the cabbie advised morosely.

'If we all thought like that, you'd be out of a job,' Crofts reasoned.

'So would my doctor, guv. Makes 'is livelihood treatin' me for stress.'

Before Crofts slammed the door she leaned towards him and whispered, 'Sure you wouldn't like me to get rid of it for you?'

He guessed she meant the gun and loved her a little more for offering to take the risk of carrying it on his behalf.

'No. I'll manage. *And* I'll be careful.'

'Today? You promised.'

'I promise. Cross my heart and hope to die . . .'

His last inane comment reminded him of Troop Sergeant Bosche again and he shut the door quickly, forcing himself to wave as the cab pulled into the stream of traffic.

Returning to his suddenly even more empty room he telephoned for coffee. When it arrived he signed the room service chit, reflecting wryly that the cost of it alone would have fed some Angolan families for a week. He knew then that he wouldn't even begin to forget Africa until he disposed of the gun.

There was a plastic carrier bag with shoes in it in the bottom of the wardrobe. Replacing the shoes with the weapon, he assessed the result critically. It looked exactly like a plastic carrier bag with a Beretta M951 pistol inside.

Pouring a black coffee he sat on the bed and brooded over the problem; it was the first time Crofts hadn't known what to do with a killing machine for thirty years. Apart from in his nightmare, anyway. Eventually he field-stripped the Beretta, breaking it down into its component parts and wrapping them in individual pieces of yesterday's *Daily Express*. When he finally added the five spare ammo clips to the bag it was as lumpy and anonymous as Saturday morning shopping.

It was only when Crofts reached the foyer again that the grim humour of his situation sank home. No London policeman would ever have imagined him to be an ex-mercenary soldier anyway, hunting for a suitable place in which to dispose of an illegal weapon. Yet they might still stop and search him once he left the hotel, for Britain's capital city was currently preoccupied by the threat posed by other anonymous visitors carrying deliberately formless packages – and particularly those who casually left them lying around. Just as Crofts was about to do.

With exquisite irony, all he'd actually managed to achieve was to disguise himself as a potential IRA bomber. Looking for a bloody target.

CHAPTER THREE

It was strange – how exposed he felt despite his mingling with the crowds emerging from Piccadilly Underground; and how easily he could convince himself that he was being watched. There seemed too many glances in his direction, lingering rather more than casual curiosity justified: the man in the red anorak, for instance; peering towards him from the other side of the ticket machines . . . surely with undue interest? And the young bloke in the motorcycle leathers lounging beside the London Transport information kiosk: casting constant, unmistakably disapproving eyes in his direction?

Until Red Anorak walked towards him, bumbled apologetically past and scrutinised the Underground destination map displayed behind Crofts with the frowning concentration of excessive myopia; while a girl carrying a crash helmet and possessed by an obvious passion for Leather Youth appeared at the head of the escalator Crofts had just ridden, and hurried across to her impatient date. And Crofts felt foolish and angry at his own ridiculous sense of guilt.

Yet the possibility that he might be under at least routine surveillance wasn't as remote as it appeared. British Special Branch did maintain a check on the movements of mercenary nationals. It wasn't unheard of for the more patriotic black sheep to be courted by certain officials who, while openly being seen to frown upon direct United Kingdom military intervention in foreign internal affairs, were still capable of initiating an arm's length operation launched by professionally discreet warsmiths.

Catching him red-handed with the current contents of his

plastic bag could well present an irresistible temptation to such specialist government servants; proving not only trying for ex-Captain Michael Crofts of the Parachute Regiment, but also representing a satisfactory saving for the less publicised expenditure of the British Treasury. To pressurise a man into the clandestine service of Her Majesty, using the threat of five years inside for being in possession of an illegal firearm, was infinitely cheaper than paying the full commercial rate for covert killing and mercenary mayhem.

Crofts hurriedly took the subway stairs to the corner of Piccadilly and Shaftesbury Avenue. This imaginative unease was a new and demoralising experience for him. Maybe it was simply engendered by the girl; the fact that for the first time he felt he'd something to lose. Maybe it really was the beginning of his psychological reintegration into lawful society – his mind finally accepting that liberty was assured not by the gun but by the denial of such personal defences. It didn't seem to matter; either way he couldn't shake off the sensation of being under constant scrutiny.

What had seemed a simple challenge at first was rapidly becoming a major exercise. He'd taken the Underground as part of a vague plan, brashly intending to dump the Beretta in some random litter bin in full view of the hurrying commuters; a characteristically defiant action for Crofts though trifling enough when set against the sum of his previous challenges to fate. Yet suddenly he was nervous – no, plain bloody scared, dammit! – to risk the myriad eyes of a public conditioned to be alert for the terror bomber in their midst.

But he kept remembering the trust the girl Pamela had shown in his promise; and sensed that their relationship might well depend on his honouring that compact.

'Bugger it!' Crofts growled aloud, and began to stride towards Cambridge Circus swinging the bag aggressively, suddenly disgusted with himself and his irrational timidity. After all, wasn't London a vast melting pot of international intrigue? No way could the security services keep tabs on any but the most immediately-menacing members of a constantly shifting population engaged in every conceivable permutation of crime, terrorism, espionage and general human vileness. Was it really likely that they would afford more than dismissive contempt for a clapped-out, second-hand soldier of fortune, posing less of a threat to the State than some eighteen-year-old kid with real Marxist hate in his belly and a home-made cigarette pack incendiary in his pocket?

Abruptly turning left into Rupert Street he worked his way into Soho. It began to rain and he became uncomfortably aware of the years he'd spent protected from the ravages of the British climate . . . but then he remembered the corpses and the brutality and the fear-sweat of his previous travels, and suddenly the London rain felt good again.

There were stalls ahead as he swung into Berwick Market. He stopped and bought a blue woollen scarf in a box. After wrapping the scarf around his neck he deliberately hesitated, the empty package in his hand. The woman serving the stall said, 'There's a dustbin behind, love, if you want to scrap it. Keep London tidy, they always tell us.'

Crofts stepped into the privacy of the stall and dropped the cardboard box, three of the spare magazines, the newspaper-wrapped barrel and the slide group assembly of the Beretta into the bin, pushing them below the waste already there. Now separated, the individual parts of the weapon would be useless to any casual finder. He called 'Thank you,' and walked on.

Without stopping he ditched the recoil spring and the remaining magazines along with an empty cigarette packet as he passed a little basket at a quiet corner. In Wardour Street he slowed to a slightly more leisurely pace past the ranks of film production offices and private cinemas until he finally sighted a pile of discarded rubbish awaiting collection, stacked in cartons outside a Greek restaurant.

Crofts did delay a moment then; feeling the already reduced weight of the gun he'd owned for half a lifetime. Oh, there was no sadness; no misplaced nostalgia . . . just an illogical guilt at destroying the last thing Troop Sergeant

Bosche's eyes had gazed upon before he died. As if it wasn't important, somehow. A trivial sacifice.

Expressionlessly he plunged the plastic bag with its remaining contents deep into a mess of kitchen scraps and walked away in his new role as a law-abiding and pacific member of society.

And became immediately aware of an unreasoning apprehension caused by *that* new sensation ahead.

When Crofts reached the bustle of Oxford Street a motorcycle drew up beside him at the junction, awaiting the lights to enter the main flow of traffic. It was only when it revved and moved off again that Crofts even spared it a passing glance.

He'd seen both riders before somewhere. Briefly. The youth with his goggles fixed firmly ahead had been standing by the Piccadilly tube information kiosk; the girl on the pillion was the one who had followed him up the escalator from the trains.

His sense of unease became even stronger. But wasn't it a bit bloody late to assume it was anything but sheer coincidence and, anyway, hadn't he just got rid of Beretta M951 so he *could* afford to ignore such idiot fantasies?

The rain stopped and the sun came out. Crofts began to drift purposelessly westwards towards Marble Arch and Hyde Park. It suddenly seemed a long afternoon ahead before six o'clock came, and Pamela Trevelyan with it.

He couldn't help wondering if the stare of Hermann Bosche would also revisit him during the forthcoming night. And, for that matter, whether the past really had been interred so easily; along with an old metallic warhorse in a pile of kitchen scraps.

He browsed aimlessly in John Lewis, bought a shirt and a pair of gloves in D. H. Evans, and found himself wandering idly through the bustle of Selfridges by lunchtime. Every so often, when he stopped to examine anything he found himself scrutinising the faces around him, looking for the suspicious factor, the rather-too-interested fellow shopper.

But there never was one. Crofts knew there wouldn't be.

Eventually he found himself rather more hungry than apprehensive and took the escalator to the upper floors. That reminded him of the crash helmet girl at Piccadilly again so he got really angry with himself, swore the hell with it and joined the queue filling into the Top Of The Shop self-service restaurant instead.

The braised chicken looked good. The girl behind the servery said 'Chips?' and Crofts shoved his plate across. 'Please.'

She added a bit more gravy and gave Crofts a smile. He grinned back and steered his tray along the rail, hoisting aboard a squashy cake and a glass of tomato juice as he shuffled. Two places ahead of him a man was ordering tea and Crofts waited patiently, unwilling to push past towards the cashier.

The man placed a stainless steel pot on his tray and began fumbling for his wallet. 'Awfully sorry to hold you up,' he excused himself politely to the small woman separating Crofts from himself.

The woman shrugged uncomprehendingly and murmured, '*Merci, M'sieu,*' while Crofts reflected how cosmopolitan London had become since his last visit. Then he glanced absently at the cause of the delay and frowned, suddenly registering remote familiarity. However it was only as the queue moved forward again that the aquiline, slightly gaunt features of the polite tea drinker finally fell into place.

The tall man headed for a vacant table while Crofts gathered cutlery and a serviette. Carrying his tray carefully he stopped before his fellow diner.

'Simpson?' he hazarded tentatively. 'You *are* Lieutenant Commander Edward Simpson, aren't you?'

The addressee hesitated, frowning up with a teaspoon poised in his hand.

'Commander now, actually. But sadly retired.' He waggled the teaspoon while his eyes narrowed reflectively; recognition a whisp away. 'Don't tell me,' he said. 'Hong Kong, was it? Or Singapore.'

'Try the Mekong Delta. Maybe eight years ago.'

Simpson's face cleared. This time he waved the spoon at Crofts with positive delight. 'Good Lord . . . Crofts? Major Crofts! It *was* Crofts, wasn't it?'

'Still is. Apart from the "Major" bit.'

'Join me, dear boy.' Simpson wriggled along the settee and patted it enthusiastically. 'Do sit down. Please.'

Crofts unloaded his meal as his newly-acquired companion turned to him. 'Not "Major" any longer, eh? A well-merited promotion, I trust?'

'Self-discharge. Through disenchantment! Anyway, rank was somewhat academic in our formation, if you'll remember – granted more by condition of contract than the Army list. We didn't exactly hold the Queen's Commission.'

'Of course,' Simpson reflected as it all came back. 'You were a somewhat informal crowd. A sort of . . . ah, self-employed security unit. Right?'

'You put it very diplomatically,' Crofts shrugged. Simpson was fully aware that the Nam boys had been hired by unspecified interests to take-out certain key Vietcong personnel north of the de-militarised zone. Where even U.S. Special Forces weren't permitted to operate.

'All governments tend to make unofficial arrangements when expediency dictates,' Simpson dismissed the matter airily.

'You should know, Commander,' Crofts retorted dryly. 'Until you and your rather-too-disciplined pirates came to pull us out, not even we knew the Royal Navy was also operating in the Mekong. On the wrong side of the line.'

'Not many chaps in the Royal Navy knew that, old boy.' The teaspoon waved cautioningly. 'Mind you – I was on extended leave at the time. Quite divorced from their Lordships of the Admiralty. Enough said?'

'The chicken looks nice,' Crofts remarked, picking up his knife and fork understandingly. 'Do you come here often, Commander?'

Crofts pushed his plate away and lit a cigarette. Since Simpson's discreet sidestep the conversation had been appropriately mundane between casual acquaintances –

about the weather, the political situation, England's prospects for the next World Cup. He was still grateful; not only had the casual meeting helped neutralise his irrational unease, but his tryst with Pamela Trevelyan was now that much closer.

'And what about you?' he asked. 'Presumably clinging to salt water in some capacity or other.'

'Lord, no,' Simpson replied without complete conviction. 'Far too old for the seaboots and sou'wester flotilla. Civil servant now, that's me. Still with Ministry of Defence, Navy, but strictly confined to sailing a desk. Bloody boring, too. Admin job. Desks awash with computer print-outs proving the country can't even afford what few grey funnel jobs we do have.'

'I'm sorry,' Crofts said. 'It must be frustrating.'

'It has its compensations, old boy. The pension's inflation-proof and at least I keep in touch with my contemporaries. Or the odd survivors left clinging tooth and nail to the active list, anyway.'

It was the first time Crofts had been given cause to remember Hermann Bosche since he'd met Simpson. 'Most of mine have got themselves blown away by now,' he found himself retorting coldly, 'or are still chasing a bullet in some half-assed bloody banana republic.'

'It was a rough game. You and that other chap – your adjutant, wasn't he? – you've shown remarkable good sense to call a halt.'

Crofts frowned doubtfully. 'Adjutant? That was Eric Harley on the Mekong job. What makes you say he's out? Last I saw of him was in Johannesburg well over a year ago. Trying to persuade Laura to let him go back to the business.'

'Laura. Presumably his wife?'

'Affirmative. They had a flat in Jo'burg. And after Delta was wiped out . . .'

'Delta?'

'An Angolan operation,' Crofts said shortly. 'Column Delta. Multi-national white mercenary force. We got chopped to pieces on a SWAPO hunt – only a few of us made it back across the border. Harley stayed on in Jo with Laura while I eventually returned here, sick of the whole bloody business. But Eric Harley's back fighting some power-crazy bastard's war, you bet on it. Unless he's dead by now.'

'He looked remarkably alive when I saw him a fortnight ago, old boy,' Simpson assured him affably. 'And there aren't that many civil wars going on in Scotland – apart from those between football supporters.'

Crofts stared at him blankly. 'Scotland! Two weeks ago?'

He thought about it for a moment, disbelief conflicting with irritation. 'But he can't be in Scotland, Simpson. He'd have let me know if he was coming to the U.K. – I left him a forwarding address.'

The aquiline features beside him reddened visibly; suddenly embarrassed. 'Sorry. Perhaps I shouldn't have . . . Oh, look, I only met him briefly in Glasgow – rather as we've done today.'

'Well, *don't* you live in a small world, then?' Crofts retorted huffily, then shrugged an immediate apology. 'Didn't mean to be snide: sorry, Simpson. Did Eric say how much time he was proposing to spend over here?'

Simpson toyed awkwardly with the teaspoon. 'I . . . ah, I rather gathered he wasn't in transit, so to speak. He seems to have settled up there permanently. Just north of Oban: placed called Auchenzie if I remember rightly.'

Crofts' brows creased in perplexity. Harley had always spent his blood money recklessly; no way could he afford to retire and live off capital. While there was only one trade for which he was equipped to earn a living . . . but – in Scotland?

'Doing what, f'r Heaven's sake?'

'Er, farming and that sort of thing, I believe.'

'Farming!'

This time Crofts really did stare. Farming! And Eric Harley? Who, through twenty years of campaigning had shown about as much concern for ecology as a Panzer division on a blitzkrieg.

Gradually he was becoming conscious of a new unease. There was something disturbing in what should merely have been a disappointing item of news gathered during his chance encounter with Commander Simpson, R.N. Retired. Crofts had known the Harleys too intimately and for too long to accept that his closest friend would have voluntarily sought the inevitable seclusion of the Scottish rural scene. They would never have left their home in the South African sun for the chill of the Northern Lights. Nor, even more significantly, would they have deliberately neglected to contact him.

Unless . . .

And that was when Crofts did identify the bleak foreboding which had persisted throughout that morning. It had been an anticipatory tremor rather than an actual threat, yet still one which could menace his so new membership of the non-violent society; which might even, as a consequence, place at grave risk his embryo and all-too-precious relationship with Pamela.

He suddenly realised that he hadn't changed, hadn't repented in the slightest. There was a certainty growing within him that should never occur in the mind of any truly reformed and peaceful man. A conviction that, when he'd naively abandoned the most faithful ally he would never have, he hadn't really offered atonement for a life of violence – he had, in fact, been committing his greatest ever folly.

And worse – Crofts wasn't even mourning for Troop Sergeant Bosche by then. Lord, no! For, faced with the imminence of what he sensed might prove a new though still-uncertain threat, already he was unashamedly regretting the sacrifice of an even more faithful companion under stress.

Called Beretta. M 951.

CHAPTER FOUR

The 380SL swallowed the northbound carriageway with little more than a self-satisfied growl. It had been Crofts' one never-regretted luxury purchase on his return to the U.K.; the Ikon gold Mercedes sports with the detachable hard top and the air of dignified breeding. He'd never owned a car before; not one of his own. Most of his transport until then had been styled in camouflaged steel with slits for windscreens and a detachable heavy machine-gun as a warning of his coming.

He wasn't enjoying the car as he should though, on that warm spring day. Even the soft mountain peaks of the Trossachs seen misting blue as he skirted the Glasgow ring road held no spark of magic; the rearing magnificence of the more northerly Grampians offered only fleeting satisfaction that his journey's end was near. For Crofts was alone, when he should have been one of two. And he was hurrying to tilt at yet another violent windmill when he should have been adopting a role of penitent sinner; a quiet man dispensing only love and gentleness.

But the Harleys *had* to be under some form of pressure. Otherwise they would never have come to Scotland without letting him know. They'd been too close, the three of them; there could only be one reason for this lack of communication – that Eric was either too proud or too concerned for Crofts' safety to involve him in whatever threat might exist.

Or had Eric finally found out? About him – and Laura. Could that be the explanation: that in some uncontrollable fit of anger she had exploded with the truth of what had once taken place between her and good old Michael bloody

Crofts, the man for whom Eric Harley had held such blind loyalty – even to the extent of offering his life?

Oh, sure, Sergeant Major Mearns had come back for him too after the Angolan massacre. Crazy Harry Mearns; living up to his legend. But Harley had been the officer, the one who made the decisions, and Crofts had never forgotten that the jungle weed and the mud creatures and a thousand other nightmare things would have been smothering more than the bones of Hermann Bosche by now, had Harley abandoned him to that gruesome battleground on the track to Chitequeta.

His hands gripped the wheel as he remembered with undiminished self-loathing. It had been an unmitigated disaster; his brief conjoining with Laura. A tearful, fumbling, unutterably sad affair which had left both of them plagued with guilt for months afterwards. Eric had stayed on in Rhodesia hunting ZAPU Terrs with the unit, while they'd flown Crofts back to Jo'burg after the shotgun blast – they weren't encouraging embarrassing mercenary casualties in the Salisbury hospitals; not that close to the inevitability of Zimbabwe independence. So naturally Laura had visited him: Christ, they'd known each other for years, hadn't they? That was when it had happened; without pre-planning, without intent, after his discharge; just a series of sweating, desperate nights punctuated with increasingly unhappy days.

Savagely Crofts booted the kick-down and the Merc whispered through eighty, ninety . . . topped the hundred mile an hour slot going into the first narrow glen road before he snarled a furious 'Stupid bastard!' and eased her back. For a brief moment he was tempted to take the easy way out; to persuade himself that Eric's resentment *was* the explanation for the Harleys' silence. In that case then maybe he'd contrived an excuse to turn around and go back to London and Pamela, and pull the sheets over his head.

Only he couldn't, and he knew it. Because it still didn't explain the reason for the Harleys' move to Scotland. And that was the real motivation behind Crofts' pilgrimage – to reinforce them in what might well be proving a time of need.

To play the role of man without honour, repaying a debt of honour.

And he'd repay it. By God he would. Even if he had to break every bone in Eric Harley's stubborn skull!

He forced himself to think about something else. Not about Pamela though: it was too unsettling to speculate on what he might have been doing with her at that moment.

Bloody Simpson, then! He began to reflect on Commander Simpson, and the previous day's ill-chance which had brought them together so briefly again. Even after leaving his lunch-time companion outside Selfridges he'd been acutely aware of the contrast between the Mekong Simpson of eight years before, and the current, rather insipid City Simpson. Had they passed by in a crowded street he would never have recognised that fleeting shadow from the past as the man he'd once met in the depths of the night in the middle of a gut-tingling oriental war.

Mind you, he'd been damn glad to meet him on that first almost-forgotten occasion . . .

He could still almost taste the terror excitement of that Nam withdrawal . . . 0400 Saigon time; the Delta a sluggish impenetrable drift of black liquid mud; the strained semi-circle of crouching breathless troopers, camouflage striped faces scanning the jungle above the dull gleam of nervously readied weapons. The cloying silence broken only by the occasional closing cry of birds which weren't birds at all but was the call sign of Vietcong Charlie. And most keenly appreciated of all, Harley's calming whisper into the handset.

'Bus Ride, Bus Ride, this is Tourist. Do you read? Over!'

A moment of exquisite tension; the steady crackle of static from the empty ether – and then the laconic, desperately-prayed-for reply.

'Tourist, this is Bus Ride. Indicate R.V. location immediate!'

Two flashes from his shaded green torch; a red spark briefly answering from the dark river . . . the long sampan prow materialising from the darkness, gliding in on the gentle swish of paddles, two prone machine-gunners angled port and starboard; a matter-of-fact English voice quietly from astern. 'Good morning, gentlemen! Anyone for boating?'

. . . but then that bloody flare! An incandescent parachute moon soaring above them, stark white and hissing. And Charlie opening up immediately, still uncertain; firing at every moving, flickering shadow . . . followed almost instantly by Sergeant Major Mearns rising recklessly from the group, legs astraddle, snarling his contempt for the others as he triggered the M16 from waist level. Bosche's *Schmeisser* abruptly racketing in concern – never graduated either, Hermann hadn't: always was as loyal to his old S.S. special as Crofts had been to the Beretta . . . and then everybody replying; chopping precisely planned segments of the jungle into whirling, ricochetting bedlam yet each already more aware that it wouldn't be enough; that Charlie has too many expendable men, and that he would still get them as they fell back on the pick-up boat without covering fire.

It was as it always seemed to have been: a bloody shambles! Every frustration in the book: thwarted at every turn. Each designated VIP hit apparently spirited away before they'd attacked. Almost as if Charlie Cong had been able to read their intentions. Sheer bloody frustration all the way through.

Until a crisp, unexpected command from the sampan's stern – 'Shoot, shoot, *shoot*!' – and, quite unbelievably, the whole of that Heath Robinson boat erupting with smoke and flame and the measured *whumph* of concealed mortars and the yammer of the bow-mounted H.M.G.'s.

Jesus, this wasn't an ordinary defensive reply, this was a whole Naval broadside! They hadn't sent a discreet little sampan in; they'd committed a miniature bloody battleship.

And that was the first time Crofts had caught sight of Simpson himself, alternately illuminated corpse-white under the flare and gristly red from the muzzle flashes of the guns. Piratical, the flickering image was: buccaneering and totally dismissive of that hellish cacophony with his bandana choker and his wide conical Vietnamese peasant hat, and

35

the only indication of his being a member of anyone's navy in the illicit White Ensign flapping defiantly from a bamboo staff astern.

But then Crofts had swung desperately to hoist Trooper Stephanakis, still struggling with the heavy field radio, into the boat . . . until a tracer round entered the back of Stephanakis' helmet and discharged most of the contents of his cranial cavity as it continued through, whereupon Crofts let him slid below the oily surface and climbed aboard himself.

From the transom twin Mercury outboards exploded into life with a roar before settling to an anxious grumble, yet still their outrageous helmsman had frowned unhurriedly over the side.

'I take it that you don't carry your dead with you, old boy?'

'Affirmative!' Mercenary Major Crofts had snarled as a line of holes stitched the planking between them. 'Jus' get us the fuck *out've* here!'

'It's a helluva way to start the day,' Lieutenant Commander Edward Simpson R.N. remarked philosophically before he finally kicked his crazy command into astern gear. And then had patted the blood-smeared thwart beside him with enormous hospitality.

'Do please consider my Wardroom entirely at your disposal *en voyage*, dear chap . . .'

And yet, eight years later, the same Simpson was merely a passing acquaintance in a bowler hat and, if the truth be told, as boring and colourless as hell. As he pushed the 380SL further north, Crofts couldn't help brooding over how ordinary Simpson had become. And got just a little frightened in the process; because it seemed that was rapidly becoming *his* ambition, too.

He'd checked in the Scottish Area telephone directory before he'd left London, and found that there was indeed a E. Harley of Den of Tarvit Farm; Auchenzie, Argyllshire. Now, as the Mercedes growled through the village itself, Crofts became more and more convinced that the Harleys *had* to be hiding from something. Lord, but it was bleak; bleak and unattractive and entirely without character. A long grey street with featureless grey houses and only the sweeping grandeur of the surrounding Highland slopes to mitigate its awfulness. There was no vibrancy of a living community about the place called Auchenzie: whatever skills and crafts had previously sustained the area must have ceased long ago; now it seemed as if hope had faded and left only a mouldering industrial chip on the shoulder of Scotland.

He passed a dilapidated garage with only the one petrol pump in the cracked forecourt. There was a Scottish crafts and tweed shop beside it, struggling bravely to inject a splash of colour in Auchenzie's monochrome palette. Then a general store, a small coffee shop, a rather smarter block of two houses with a blue *Police* sign in the neat front garden, a once white-painted hotel chipped by the winter frosts and two faded stars of indifference to mark its status; a fishing tackle and gunsmith's window which looked as though its owner had fished or shot everything that swam or ran and then just closed up and emigrated, and a sub-post office. And that, apart from the drab terraced houses, was the sum total of the Burgh of Auchenzie.

An impressively substantial rosy-cheeked woman was backing down the post office steps hauling a pram. No alternative source of information being apparent Crofts slid the Merc alongside her and leaned out.

'Excuse me, but could you direct me to Den of Tarvit farm, please?'

She turned and eyed the car, but her expression didn't change. It was still one of flustered intolerance with babies, sub-post office steps and the complex logistic problems associated with supporting whatever family she had, and all that in the middle of nowhere.

'See yon government family allowance they gie you for the bairns?' she demanded accusingly. 'Would you no' think it was time for them to make it keep up wi' the inflation?'

Crofts frowned and considered the point. He'd never thought about an inflating baby before. 'Probably. I don't suppose it is very much, not with prices the way they are.'

'It's an absolute damn scandal,' the woman snapped, and began to tuck the bedding around the child with seemingly lethal, karate-like finger stabs. Crofts hoped she wouldn't miss the blankets and solve at least part of her child allowance requirement in one go.

'Er . . . the farm?' he remined her tentatively. 'Den of Tarvit, according to the telephone directory.'

'It's no' a farm,' the fearsome lady adjudicated. 'It's naething but scrappit land and peat marsh. And gey run-down at that.'

'I'd still like to find it,' Crofts said almost pleadingly and not without a certain awe of his unexpected adversary.

'Half a mile down this road. Turn left and gang doon past the auld quarry for maybe two mile. It's the coast road so you'll find it if ye dinnae drive yerself clear intae the sea instead.'

'Thank you very much,' Crofts said hurriedly and began to ease the car ahead. But the woman clamped an imperious fist on the door frame and he hit the brake in case she tore it off.

He wasn't thinking of the appalling woman's hand, either. His apprehension was for the Mercedes' door.

'Are you no' fae England?' she demanded suspiciously.

'Er . . . yes,' he admitted cautiously. 'Does it matter?'

'Maybe no',' she retorted through pursed, disapproving lips. 'Maybe they'll let *you* in, seeing you're one of them and driving a smart motor car besides.'

Crofts frowned, intrigued despite his desire to escape. 'You mean they discourage visitors?'

'They threatened my Tam wi' a *shotgun*, so they did! Told him tae stay away or next time they'd hae him for poaching – and him just out for a wee rabbit or two tae help wi' the family allowance.'

'They? You mean Mr and Mrs Harley said that?'

'Not the lady. She's a couthie enough wee lass . . . but yon Harley's no' well liked around here. Nor yon he calls his grieve.'

'Grieve?' Crofts queried uncertainly.

'Och aye, you're English sure enough,' the woman confirmed with enormous contempt, releasing the Mercedes and grasping the handles of the pram as if preparing to steer it into action instead. 'It's your English government that's doing it, ye ken? Holding back the family allowances fae guid Scots bairns . . .'

He drove all the way to the turn-off before he dared slow down. Whoever or, come to that, whatever threatened Eric Harley could surely prove only a pale shadow of the Ferocious Mother of Auchenzie Village. For the first time since he'd met Simpson in London, Crofts smiled.

It was significant, though. About her Tam, and the shotgun. But what the hell was a *grieve*?

He saw her as he carefully eased the car through the yard gate, thankful that Teutonic engineering and suspension had survived a cross country lane designed to tax the durability of a half-tracked personnel carrier.

She was hanging washing on a scrap of line strung from the house to the trunk of a weathered tree. A few disconsolate fowls picked gloomily around the sagging barn while an ancient John Deere tractor mouldered quietly behind the remains of a drystane dyke.

Before she even turned he could see she looked as tired and drab as her environment. Any doubts he'd previously held were well and truly dissipated – whatever their reasons for living like this, they were never through choice of Laura Harley.

He got out of the car and walked up behind her. She carried on clipping pegs and called, 'With you in a minute, Mister McKay. We'll only need mince today; maybe a nice piece of pork.'

Crofts said, 'Hello, Laura.'

She froze, one hand still raised to the line. Her voice held only the slightest tremor. 'I thought . . . it was Mister McKay, the butcher.'

He smiled softly. 'I'm sorry. Though maybe you could order a little more when he does come. Now you've got a guest for dinner.'

She did turn then, and even as she did he felt the old pleasure in looking at her return as powerfully as ever. Despite the creases shadowing her eyes she was still striking. Even in the faded jeans and the thick Shetland jersey and the bloody awful atmosphere of that decrepit place, Eric's wife and his own frustrated love looked as desirable as he remembered.

'Mike,' she whispered. 'Ohhhh, *Mike!*'

As soon as she threw her arms around him and clung to him and began to cry, he was happy to dismiss what had proved one of the most worrying fears he had endured through the previous hours — that Laura Harley might indeed have confessed to Eric about their long-dead and shameful affair. To have done that would have been to invite a rift between himself and her which could never have been bridged by any tears.

And there was no rift. For that, at least, Crofts felt very grateful.

'Eric will be back soon,' Laura offered eventually between sniffs and a great dabbing of eyes. She made coffee for them both and they waited in the warm and surprisingly pleasant kitchen of the farmhouse, talking and, occasionally, even lightly touching the backs of one another's hand as if to assure each other that they were still friends. No more than that though; both of them knew there never could be. Not again.

Yet there was an imperceptible wariness all the same, for Crofts avoided the obvious questions while she neither encouraged nor broached them. And because of that manifest omission, the certainty that she *was* withholding something grew stronger within him.

It couldn't be allowed to go on. Abruptly he placed his hand more firmly over hers and held her gaze.

'Why didn't you let me know you were living up here?'

She didn't drop her eyes. It was almost as if she had been anticipating him. 'Because we both love you,' she said simply.

Crofts squeezed her fingers gently. 'Thank you. But it doesn't answer the question, does it?'

'How *did* you find out, anyway?'

He smiled, aware that she was still trying somewhat artlessly to divert him. 'Chap called Simpson. He'd met Eric in Glasgow and mentioned it to me.'

She frowned slightly. Obviously the name meant nothing to her.

'Just an old acquaintance. We'd all been together once. Briefly, a long time ago . . . Why *are* the two of you living here, Laura?'

'Would you believe me if I said we liked it?'

'No! It's a dump. And it gets bloody cold in the winter.'

'I know,' she said sombrely. 'We've already survived part of one.'

'You've been here that long?' he asked in surprise.

'Not me; I only came over about six weeks ago. Eric's been here since last November.'

'But *why*?' Crofts insisted. 'Why the move; why the secrecy? Christ, Eric knows I'd help if he'd got into some sort of trouble.'

'He also knew you'd decided to give up the . . . well, the business you were both involved in, Mike.'

'Which implies that he *hasn't*! Is that the reason for the silence, Laura – to prevent me from getting involved: to protect me against myself?'

She began to cry again and suddenly he understood how much the strain had told on her, even in six weeks, and got angry with Eric for inflicting this on the one person he cherished so dearly.

'Is Eric back in the mercenary trade, and crazy enough to try something in Scotland, Laura?' he pressed on grimly. 'Or is it a question of the past catching up. Has *he* been threatened?'

'I don't know!' she sobbed. 'Please, Mike – I don't KNOW, and that's what makes me so frightened. He's changed, Mike: we came here because I thought he really did want to, but since then he's been under increasing pressure in some way; nervous, irritable. I get the impression he's even scared, sometimes. But he's never let me get in touch with you and I know it's only because he doesn't want you involved.'

A vehicle drew up outside the house and the diesel rumble of the engine cut. Crofts recognised the slam of a Land Rover door and Laura began to dry her eyes quickly, apprehensively.

'I'm not going to go away, you know,' he said doggedly. 'Not now. Not now I'm here.'

It was her turn to squeeze his hand. Quickly. One last time before Eric came in.

'I don't want you to, Mike. I know he needs help, and perhaps you – we – owe it to him. Please stay. Even though he hates you for it.'

But that time Crofts didn't answer, because in the final moments of waiting for Eric he had been absently watching the mountainside through the tiny kitchen window. And just as the familiar footsteps entered the hall, he registered a brief but unmistakable spark against the peat-brown lower slopes.

The flash of lowering sun against optically convex glass. A soldier's warning of distant surveillance – or some Highland ornithologist at play in his natural habitat?

But if Den of Tarvit Farm *was* under observation, then was that anonymous watcher out there because of Eric Harley's arrival? Or because of his own?

CHAPTER FIVE

They gazed at each other for a long time after Eric halted abruptly in the doorway. Crofts didn't get up; just sat there grinning and with a quizzical lift to his eyebrow, while the most unlikely farmer on the Argyll coast registered an involuntary delight which, Crofts was quick to notice, changed to growing bewilderment, even hostility before he finally found words.

'How the hell did you know we were here?'

'Why the hell did I have to find out by accident?' Crofts retorted unabashed. 'Hello, Eric. I'm glad you're pleased to see me.'

'Jesus,' Harley said, coming forward at last. 'It *is* good, Mike. I'm sorry! We're not used to surprises up here.'

Crofts stood up and gripped the outstretched hand firmly; interrogatively. 'You really sure, Eric – no surprises at all?'

Harley looked him straight in the eye. 'You've lost your Africa tan, old son,' he rejoined smoothly.

'Tea or coffee, darling?' Laura asked with only the faintest trace of unease.

And so the three of them talked of things past; of Africa and mutual friends, and of Crofts' still vague plans for his retirement and of nostalgic memories in general. He didn't mention Pamela Trevelyan though, nor the real reason for his sitting in that comfortable room with them, while Eric never commented on having moved to Scotland or even asked why Crofts was there – it was all so bloody sterile and unlike the old times that he was almost relieved when Harley stretched and rose from his chair.

'Fantastic to see you again, Mike. Really! Look, I've got

to run into the village for odds and sods. Why don't you come with me – quick recce of the family estate *en route* – and back for dinner before you push on to wherever you're bound?'

'Eric!' Laura blurted out in involuntary outrage.

Crofts smiled beatifically. 'Terrific. Only I'm not actually heading for anywhere. I've come especially to see the two of you.'

Harley's expression tightened and this time there was no concealing the apprehension. 'What the hell for?'

'Twenty years of being bloody miserable in the mud alongside you, fellow Major. And because I love your wife nearly as much as you do . . . an' why the hell not, huh? Anyway, maybe I might even fancy being a farmer too, some time.'

'Crap!' Eric growled, with a flash of the old spirit.

'Yes: *isn't it?*' Crofts retorted pointedly.

Harley ran his hand through his hair uncertainly and looked embarrassed. 'It's . . . well, it's a bad time, old boy. Seeds to be sown, fences to be mended . . .'

'You can say that again, about the fences! Along with a few other minor construction projects as well – like replacing roofs an' roads.'

'We don't have any spare beds. We're even putting the boys . . .'

'Boys?'

'The farm staff – we're even boarding them temporarily in the Auchenzie pub while the old cottages are being restored.'

'Then you're a bloody sight richer than you deserve,' Crofts snapped, irritated despite himself. 'Anyway, shouldn't you really say, "When the old cottages *start* to be restored"? If you mean the ones I passed coming down here they haven't seen a workman since the Highland bloody Clearances!'

'STOP IT!' Laura finally exploded. 'Stop it, both of you! There *is* a bed and you know it, Eric. It's only empty because I won't share our house with those . . . those men you employ.'

'Or I can stay in the pub with 'em,' Crofts supplemented unabashed. 'And work like an Irish navvy for a few days to help out.'

'That won't be necessary, thank you,' Eric said with cold precision.

Crofts shrugged philosophically. 'O.K.! So I live like a leech instead. Bed and breakfast in the Auchenzie Hilton and Laura can cook my dinners.'

'You'll stay here, Mike, and that's final,' Laura stipulated with a defiant glare at her husband. 'I'm sorry. I don't know what's got into him.'

Harley reached for his coat and crammed his old army beret on his head. 'I'll wait for you in the Rover,' he growled bitterly. 'While my wife apologises for me!'

Crofts waited until he'd slammed the door, then kissed Laura gently on the cheek. 'You're right. He is running scared.'

She clung to him for a long unhappy moment. 'So am I. You will stay, won't you, Mike? And find out why?'

He grinned with an assurance he didn't feel. 'They'll have to shoot me to stop me, Mrs Harley.'

But he didn't mean it quite the way it sounded. Not when he didn't even have a gun any more. And particularly when, as he left the farmhouse, he saw once again the flash of watching glasses from the mountain.

Eric had already started the Rover when Crofts climbed in and intoned, 'Drive on, MacDuff!'

'Ha bloody ha!' the discomfited husband growled. Crofts grinned.

'Remember the last time – Angola? You were a damn sight more insistent on my crawling aboard then, and I've never ceased to thank my lucky stars you were, pal.'

But then he also remembered *why* he'd delayed his withdrawal from that particular nightmare, and saw again the phantom tortured face of Hermann Bosche briefly staring up at him in place of the Rover dashboard, and suddenly his cheerful mask slipped a little.

They drove for a time in silence, but he didn't need a

running commentary to note that very little work, either maintenance or agricultural, had been carried out on Den of Tarvit Farm during the Harley's tenancy. That factor alone gave him cause for reflection: Eric had claimed only to have rented the property which – while it did explain how he might have overcome his lack of capital – equally emphasised the illogicality of his not then endeavouring to milk every possible source of income in the coming season.

Surely odd? For an allegedly determined newcomer to the soil.

Eventually Eric did have the grace to wriggle awkwardly behind the wheel. 'Oh, look, I know I should've written. Kept meaning to, of course, Mike. But as a matter of interest, how . . . ah . . . how *did* you find out we were up here anyway?'

'Simpson told me. Remember Simpson?'

'*Simpson?*'

Crofts frowned at his companion. Eric Harley's surprise seemed a bit overdone to say the least.

'Yeah – Simpson,' he confirmed. 'Vietnam Simpson: the oddball sailorman who pulled us out of the Mekong operation. He said he'd met you in Glasgow a few weeks back an' . . .'

'I *know* which Simpson!' Eric retorted and then shrugged lamely. 'A bit surprised, that's all – at his running into both of us after all this time. Seems a hell of a coincidence.'

'Set your mind at rest. I was the one who recognised Simpson; he wouldn't even have noticed me if I hadn't approached him.'

They were nearly at the section where the track ran along the edge of the cliffs before Eric spoke again, more intimately this time; more as they used to be.

'All right, Mike. This isn't just a social visit – why *did* you come all the way up here?'

Crofts eyed him expressionlessly. 'Shouldn't I be the one asking that? You're no frustrated tiller of the sod, friend: you know it and I know it. Hell, man, you've always been more in your element planning a field of fire than a field of hay. Are you hiding from something up in this bloody

46

wilderness, Eric? Some form of threat?'

Eric didn't answer immediately, he simply drove the Land Rover on to the verge and stopped, frowning distantly at the road ahead. It was very quiet up there a hundred feet above the sea; only the gentle sigh of breaking waves on the rocks below, and the call of seabirds and the distant drone of a tractor broke the Highland stillness. Crofts sat patiently and waited for his friend to speak; gazing down over the cliff edge to where the waves of centuries had eroded a long, narrow cleft into the land, and to where not-quite-so ancient Highlandmen had once capitalised on its natural protection by extending a jetty part way across the seaward entrance to form a tiny harbour. Only now the sea was reclaiming that too, as its irregular, collapsing granite buttresses showed.

Finally Harley turned to face him.

'Go away, Mike,' he said quietly. 'Just go back to London and forget Auchenzie.'

Crofts eyed him, placidly. 'Just like that?'

'Just like that! I'm sorry.'

'Why?'

Eric slammed his hand on the back of the seat in frustration. 'Jesus Christ! O.K., Mike; I've been trying to avoid this – but maybe I feel it's you who poses the threat. Maybe *I'm* the one who wants out; wants to cut all links with the old days. To keep away from everything an' everyone connected with the past. And maybe that includes a certain Major Crofts who may, or then again, may NOT have reformed!'

'Maybe – but does it?'

Crofts gazed levelly at Eric for a long time, until the defiant glare became uncertain and his friend's eyes finally dropped. Then he punched him gently on the shoulder and reached for the door handle.

'Let's go for a walk, huh? Throw stones in the water, catch a few crabs down there in the rocks. I'm here for a few days, whether invited or not, so humour me, Eric. Call it a soldier's swansong, if you like; to a very long comradeship.'

Harley said, 'You haven't changed. You're still a pigheaded bastard, aren't you?'

He didn't mean it harshly: there was a fondness there. Yet, somehow, an indefinable sadness as well.

Despite Eric's protestations that there really wasn't time they did finally scramble down the crumbling steps to the little cove. Crofts threw a few stones into the clear water as he stared idly about him. It was a picture book harbour; a fragment of the real, beautiful Scotland yet one which, like Auchenzie itself, had fallen prey to the disease of progress.

But at one time it had fulfilled a useful function: there was some primitive form of hoist or derrick abandoned high on the cliff top above, now reduced to a rusting iron skeleton staring blankly out over the sea; while on the knuckle of the pier itself an equally ancient manual crane still pointed a mouldering finger to the sky. Crofts wondered what manner of industry could have demanded such Victorian technology in this rural place.

'The old quarries,' Eric explained vaguely. 'They used to ship a lot of the stone for the great buildings around Glasgow from here, I believe. They'd bring it to that upper gantry on horse-drawn carts, then lower the dressed blocks to the jetty where they craned them aboard steam puffers up from the Clyde.'

Crofts began to pick his way along the jetty itself, careful not to slip between the sagging shoulders of the displaced stones which formed it. Piles of dried seaweed straggled as a reminder of the recent winter gales. Absently he picked a strand and popped each seed case as he wandered on; just like he'd done as a child on holiday, so many almost forgotten years before.

Eric's caution came sharp from the beach. Ever since they'd descended he'd been like a cat on hot bricks, agitating to get away. 'Stay off there. All I need now is you with a broken ankle. Come on, Mike! I want to get up to the village before the store closes.'

Crofts stopped and lit a cigarette, taking a long time over it and casually eyeing the old crane as he did.

'Come *on*!' Harley called again, more urgently this time. Crofts turned and accidentally dropped his cigarette packet, bending stiffly to retrieve it from where it had fallen against one of the rusted mooring rings.

'Fabulous little harbour,' he said as he walked back. 'Do they still work the quarries, then?'

Eric began to head for the steps back up to the track, impatient to be gone. 'Not for decades. They closed down before the First World War according to the locals. It's just a page of history now, this cove.'

'Never used at all? Not even by local yachts?'

'It's private,' Harley retorted shortly. 'I don't encourage weekend sailors. Besides, it's too bloody dangerous to enter without local knowledge; the leading marks which gave the puffers their approach have long gone an' I'm too busy to replace 'em for tourists.'

'Perhaps you'll need to, one day. When you can afford a luxury yacht of your own,' Crofts suggested as he scrambled in the wake of his reluctant guide. 'Look, old boy: I don't particularly want to spend more time sitting in a motor car today. Point me towards the farm and I'll stretch my legs going back while you do your thing in the village.'

'Please yourself,' Harley shrugged, obviously nettled by the time he'd already wasted. Then he pulled a face, wryly apologetic for his abruptness.

'Look,' he said awkwardly, gesturing inland. 'That mountain over there's called Ben Quilhadder; about two thousand metres as the crow flies. At the foot of it, and running parallel to this coast is the main north road – I'll drive back from Auchenzie that way; stroll across and I'll pick you up in, say, an hour?'

Crofts glanced at his watch and saluted elaborately. 'R.V. main road, eighteen-thirty Zulu. Roger!'

'Forget the procedure, pal – I'm a farmer now,' Eric grinned as he slammed the Rover door. Before he drove off he leaned out and jerked a thumb at the old harbour. 'But don't go back down there, Major. Not on your own. An' that is an order!'

'Forget orders too, pal: *I'm* a civilian now,' Crofts retorted cheerfully. 'But I won't, anyway. I've seen all there is to be seen.'

He watched until the Land Rover was out of sight, then walked across to where the venerable iron hoist reared high above the little cove, examining it thoughtfully. It was still remarkably well preserved under its scale of peeling rust, though whatever tackles had originally existed to handle the stone blocks had long been removed or had crumbled to dust.

He didn't attempt to retrace his steps down to the jetty, but then he didn't need to break his promise to Eric on that score – he really *had* seen as much as he needed to already. Now only a few explanations seemed called for.

Because why – when, according to Harley, no present day craft ever entered the tiny harbour at Den of Tarvit Farm – were the rusted mooring rings friction-bright on their inner circumference, almost as though the warps of a short-swinging vessel had very recently polished away the patina of years?

And even more intriguingly, how – when the last quarry-man must have left Auchenzie long before Crofts and Harley were born – could the old manually operated crane at the pierhead still bear traces of fresh grease around all its working parts?

As well as having been fitted with a brand new lifting wire. Replaced so recently, in fact, that not even the guano of the countless seabirds wheeling above had been given time to settle in its coils.

It was a beautiful spring evening with the merest Highland chill to the air as he headed cross-country for the base of Quilhadder. Apart from occasional patches of peat bog squelching underfoot the ground was dry and flat, hummocks of coarse dune grass and thistle echoing the creak of grasshoppers and the plaintive warnings of nesting birds. There was hardly any wind and to his left he could detect a fine haze rising from the barely visible chimneys of Den of Tarvit Farm. He began to think how nice it would have been if he'd brought Pamela Trevelyan after all: had ignored the oppressive unease which had caused him to come north alone; the sense of impending violence that had mounted from the moment when Simpson first dropped his innocent bombshell.

She'd wanted to come: hadn't she practically pleaded with him that evening when he met her in the Rooftop Lounge? All big, wide eyes full of anticipation when he'd told her he had to drive north for a few days on unexpected business – and sweet petulance when he'd insisted on travelling alone.

He hadn't lied to her – not really. He didn't ever want to do that. But he hadn't told her the whole truth either: that it was actually his own decision and not a telephone call from a very close ex-service comrade which had been instrumental in his going.

'Bought a run-down hill farm or something . . .' He hadn't been *that* far from the truth there, either! 'Got himself in a mess, though – over his head financially. Wants me to guarantee a further loan from the bank to stop him going under altogether. I'm morally bound to go and at least take a look at the bloody place.'

'But why alone?' she'd pouted, disappointment bright in her eyes. 'Why can't we go up there together. Wouldn't your Eric put us up for a few nights?'

'It's a shambles as far as I know. Whole place falling to bits.' Lord, he *had* been predicting the future with uncanny accuracy. 'Probably not even a decent room without a pig or something in it.'

'I like pigs,' Pam had retorted, then had allowed her knee to touch his under the table. 'And anyway, all we need is a bed. A double bed.'

'NO!' he'd protested desperately. 'Dammit, the bloke's practically living under canvas. It's front line stuff: mud an' freezing Scottish mountain weather, and miles from civilisation; even from the Auchenzie place.'

She'd gazed at him rather oddly for quite a long time after that. Wondering. He'd been tortured with the fear that she might have suspected another woman's involvement . . . but he *couldn't* explain any further. He couldn't have told her the real truth – that all his senses warned him Eric Harley was under threat, and that any kind of threat which came as a legacy from the mercenary game could well prove the nine millimetre kind.

And Crofts would rather have lost Pamela Trevelyan altogether than risk her facing an experience like that.

He hadn't gone far before he crested a slight incline and slowed his pace briefly, intrigued. A cluster of low buildings reared ahead, grouped geometrically behind a taller, vaguely familiar structure. At first glance he could see they were long abandoned, with cement-rendered walls now shedding in great ugly patches, and only the collapsing frames without glass to identify what had once been metal windows. Stretching across the foreground ran a wide swathe of concrete hardstand which, like the huts, had yielded to the encroachment of sand and dune grass and the cracking frosts of years.

Perhaps it was the loneliness, the romantic isolation of that forgotten place, but Crofts approached what could only have been the control tower of a derelict Second World War airfield with a sense of childish reverence. How many ghosts of flying men – adults when he had been but a child – now drifted among these isolated ruins? How many crews had winged aloft from here with mock casualness set on their masked faces and a fear-sick dryness in their throats?

The runway had survived remarkably well, with the reinforced surface splitting only where vegetable forces had finally wriggled their way towards the light. Here and there the trunks of rowan and baby fir had actually taken root in the fissures – solitary triumphs of nature over man – while great tangles of gorse filled the dispersal bays and piled within the hangar frame stripped of corrugated cladding.

He peered inside the doorless entrance to the control tower as he picked his way among the sombre ruins; conscious of the need to press on towards the road and his rendezvous with Harley but unable to resist one peek through the mists of recent time.

There was an old plough dimly seen blocking the rotted internal stairway. A pile of flattened tinder-dry straw, as if some animal had at one time been quartered there; several bales of hay; a battered shovel, coils of rusted wire. Crofts frowned at the wire for a few moments: it was very old, and could well have been discarded from a certain jetty crane not a million miles from there.

A faded drawing still remained on the mildew peeling wall; a stylised seabird diving towards a wind-whipped sea, illustrated in the form of a crest. The crayoned letters were barely decipherable after the intervening years – 814 SQUADRON: COASTAL COMMAND. There were other scrawled legends too, with less official status: *Wot, no girls? Look out, Adolph – Charlie W's finally learned to fly! Pilot Officer Rankine pranged here.* And an enigmatic, *Arthur likes Ernie.*

Crofts found himself grinning as he withdrew from that silent, spectral place. Until he remembered the discarded wire, and began to wonder why yet again.

The mountain, Ben Quilhadder, towered above him when he finally reached the road. He was eight minutes early, so he stood for a few seconds staring up. It was from those rocky slopes that the flashes had betrayed the anonymous watcher. He wondered if whoever had caused them might still be there. It was impossible to tell though: the road had been cut into the mountainside on that stretch and only the upper slopes, still streaked with gulley snow, were visible above the high embankment.

As he idled, waiting for Eric, he heard a heavy vehicle approaching from behind and stepped cautiously back from the verge: even for the Scottish Highlands it was a narrow road. A lorry rounded the bend heading north and as it did so the driver raised a hand in casual salute. Crofts returned the politeness as the truck rumbled out of sight again, casually noting as it passed the words ROYAL NAVY stencilled on its dark blue side. They reminded him of Simpson and he sniffed irritably. Bloody Simpson! If it hadn't been for Simpso . . .

The crash and the squeal of brakes shattered the mountain stillness without warning: slashing starkly across the evening peace. Instantly Crofts whirled back towards

Auchenzie, guessing with chill precision that it couldn't concern the Navy truck – that must now be well ahead, while the shriek of tortured rubber was coming from *behind*.

... and then came the second grating squeal of metal against rock: a shocked lament of skipping, fading echoes across the mountain. And finally, silence once again.

Even as Crofts began running there was already a grim certainty within him. Somehow, he *knew* the incident must involve Eric Harley.

Long before he actually came upon the tailboard of the Tarvit Land Rover. See-sawing with balance-scale delicacy over the slowly crumbling edge of a fifty foot drop.

CHAPTER SIX

The track had been carved into the side of the mountain at the point where the Rover was on the verge of becoming airborne. The lower slope of Quilhadder had been blasted to form the vertical rock face of the cutting itself, the narrow shelf of road and, finally, at the point where Eric Harley's vehicle balanced with such hair-raising precision, a virtually sheer drop to the bed of a mountain burn.

Crofts skidded to a momentary halt. Only the hush of the evening and the glass-tinkle excitement of running water from below competed with the harsh pumping of his own lungs – and the more leisurely, metronome creak of the finely poised Land Rover with its driver slumped motionless over the wheel.

The windscreen had disintegrated, Crofts could see that instantly: and at the point of initial impact, judging by the trail of sparkling fragments leading back along the road. Harley still didn't move as he approached with grimly disciplined caution, apprehensive of disturbing the fragile balance. Seen from behind there was blood on the side of Eric's face and twinkles of glass frosting the hunched shoulders of his tattered combat jacket, but no sign of a major wound. Like, say, the fist-sized exit cavity of a high-velocity sniper's bullet might have left.

Eric called quietly, still without moving. 'Something heavy went through the screen. I lost her on the bloody bend.'

'Ah,' Crofts retorted with acid surprise. 'I naturally assumed you drove like that all the time.'

55

And felt warm and happy inside because Eric wasn't dead after all.

'I'd like to get the hell out of this seat, if you don't mind,' Harley growled, still not daring to budge. 'Except the whole bloody lot's likely to go over if I rock the boat – with me still in it!'

More loose scree on the lip broke away and went skipping and tumbling down to the stream. The stern of the Rover began to rise before Crofts recklessly flung himself forward, grabbing the tailgate and feeling very frightened for Eric again.

'Jesus!' Harley choked.

'I'm going to climb aboard,' Crofts stated with icy calm. 'To counterbalance you . . .'

'Don't be bloody stupid! She could take you over as well then,' Eric snarled, and Crofts could see his blood-streaked knuckles tight-white as they gripped the wheel.

'No, she won't,' he reassured the see-saw man. 'If she starts to slide I'll get off again. No point in us both suffering.'

Gently he eased himself astride the tailgate. Even with his added weight the rear wheels barely brushed the ground. Inch by nerve-racking inch Eric Harley began to lever himself over the back of the bench seat.

'You get a lovely view from up here,' Crofts remarked as his precarious perch began to pendulum unsteadily.

Then closed his eyes. Very tightly indeed.

'That's where the bloody thing must've rolled from,' Eric said a few minutes later, gazing up at the high face of the mountain cut. After securing the tail of the Rover they had walked back to where the first splinters of windscreen glass spattered the road.

Crofts squinted sourly against the evening sun. 'What makes you think it rolled? There's no sign of any other subsidence. One rock doesn't make an avalanche.'

Harley dabbed an ineffectual hankie at the blood trickling from his gnashed forehead. 'An' what does *that* mean?'

Crofts headed back towards the vehicle. The granite

boulder still lay in the passenger well where it had tumbled after shattering the screen. 'It means I think someone's been trying to kill you. Accidentally!'

Eric halted abruptly, his face set tightly under the mask of blood. Too tightly. 'Don't be bloody silly!'

Crofts lifted the stone and hefted it pointedly. 'If I wanted to eliminate someone and make it look like an accident; an' if I expected that particular someone to drive along this particular road at this particular time; and if I *also* knew he'd be doing, say, fifty round the bends because he's an irresponsible bastard behind a wheel – then I'd be tempted to drop a rock on him. Just like this one.'

'Except for one thing – apart from the idiocy of your basic assumption,' Eric growled uncertainly. 'They'd have had to know I *was* expected to use this road at this particular time. And they couldn't have, could they?'

'Oh, yes they could,' Crofts contradicted him placidly. 'Because whoever it is has been watching us all afternoon: and it didn't take the mind of a genius to guess which way you'd return after you left me to go into Auchenzie.'

He wished he'd been allowed a little longer to analyse the disturbed expression in Harley's eyes before the mask came down again and Eric took the rock from his hand, throwing it out and over the drop until it fell with a splash into the stream.

'Look, are you goin' to help or not?' he growled, gesturing irritably towards the see-saw vehicle.

'That,' Crofts retorted, turning away in temporary defeat, 'is what I've been *trying* to bloody do ever since I came!'

He never raised the subject again; not even after they'd recovered the otherwise undamaged Rover and were driving back to the farm. Whether Eric was deliberately avoiding further questions or had merely slipped into one of his inexplicable strained silences was rapidly becoming irrelevant. There was no rapport between them any longer; no fraternal feeling. Harley had made it plain that whatever was happening was no concern of his one-time friend – his vehement denial that there had been any possibility of foul play in the recent 'accident' had finally and clumsily underlined that.

Yet the afternoon had already justified the unease which had niggled Crofts ever since his meeting with Simpson. If the levitated rock had been caused by human agency, then Eric Harley undoubtedly *was* involved in some deep and dangerous game; and whatever evil marred the derelict beauty of Den of Tarvit Farm was being generated not by Eric's past but by Eric's current actions. The signs of recent activity at the old jetty had convinced him of that, reinforced as they were by Harley's anxiety to discourage him from closer inspection.

It was only when they'd entered the farmyard and Eric had stopped the Rover that he spoke for the first time, and then only with diffidence. 'Look, old boy, I'd . . . well, I'd rather you didn't say anything to Laura about what happened.' ·

'An' I'm not bloody surprised,' Crofts snapped, unable to contain his growing resentment. 'You haven't exactly said hellish much to me about it either.'

'So what's there to say? It was an accident,' Harley muttered doggedly.

Crofts clambered out of the vehicle, then swung aggressively to face Eric. 'Yeah, so you keep reminding me . . .'

He hesitated, fighting the hurt which kept welling inside him – and failing. Bitterly he turned away. 'Maybe you'd better hide this wreck in the barn, chum. I suppose you can claim those cuts happened when you tripped over your bloody halo – always assuming, of course, that you're better at lying to your wife than you are to me!'

He sensed the need for caution even as he entered the kitchen. Oh, Laura was waiting and obviously pleased to see him back yet there was a wariness there as well. She spoke hurriedly before he did, warning him, yet still managing to convey her distaste.

'The grieve's waiting to see Eric, Mike – that means our foreman, up here. With the other boys who work the farm.'

So at least Crofts had learned something that afternoon:

now he knew what the Ferocious Mother of Auchenzie had meant by a 'grieve'. Regrettably that wasn't all he learned, for – as the tallest of the four men lounging at the table rose and threw an openly mocking salute towards him – he discovered that whatever trouble Eric Harley *had* got himself into promised to be more violent, more sinister, than any conceived even during Crofts' worst moments of apprehension.

When the most improbable grieve of Tarvit Farm smiled the ice-chip smile that Crofts hadn't seen for a long time. Not, in fact, since the mutilation called Hermann Bosche had gazed so pleadingly into the muzzle of his Beretta from that offal-strewn slaughter ground in Angola.

'Nice to see you again. *Sir*!' Harry Mearns grinned.

Ex-Company Sergeant Major Mearns, late of the late Column Delta.

CHAPTER SEVEN

After the evening meal Crofts somewhat reluctantly took the Mercedes back along that suspension-torturing track towards the main Auchenzie road with the intention of ringing Pam Trevelyan. He didn't quite know why he'd hesitated to use the telephone at the farm. Hell, what was so embarrassing about his infatuation with a girl; even one less than half his age? Weren't there already too many secrets driving an ever-widening gulf between Eric and him?

Between the Harleys themselves, come to that. Obviously Laura hadn't been aware of Harley's previous connection with Harry Mearns: it wasn't surprising – if he'd been Eric Harley *he* wouldn't have wanted to tell his wife about a professional acquaintance like Harry, even under normal circumstances. And these were hardly normal circumstances.

But what with his own preoccupation with the reappearance of Harry Mearns – supported, incidentally, by a bunch of neanderthals who made your average Mafia hit man look like a Jesuit missionary – and the wall of sullen defensiveness presented by Harley as they ate, Crofts felt he had to get away, even if only to brood darkly.

He only found one callbox in the village, defaced with scrawled legends informing an uninterested public that *Eck loves Jessie* and *MacAlister wis here* and the arrogant assurance, *Govan Huns OK!* It illustrated all too clearly that Auchenzie was within day trip reach of the spray-can morons fae Glasgae.

She answered immediately when the hotel switchboard put him through. He couldn't help feeling a warm gratitude:

he'd said he would try and phone about eight, but she was young and far too attractive; it would have been so easy for her to have gone out and made excuses later. Even to have forgotten that he was ringing at all.

'I've missed you,' she said, and he very much wanted to believe her.

'I've missed you, too.'

'Well, *is* there a pig in your room?'

He frowned momentarily, then grinned into the mouthpiece. 'No. But there's a fearsome Scottish lady on the loose who eats Londoners; and getting down to the farm needs the logistic support of an Anapurna expedition.'

She laughed, but it only made her seem even further away.

'Are you coming back tomorrow?' she asked with a childishly endearing directness. He didn't have to try hard to convey his frustration.

'It may take a few days. Eric's a terrible farmer. I've more or less promised to stay until we sort things out.'

She didn't say anything for a moment and he began to worry again. Then her voice came back with deliberate casualness. 'What sort of things, Michael?'

Crofts traced his reflection in the broken kiosk mirror. 'Oh, you know – *things*. Accounts; bank managers; broken-down tractors an' . . . well . . . things.'

Her next gambit, when it came, was as gratefully received as it proved morale-shattering.

'Can you guess what I'm doing now?' she asked. Very softly indeed.

He frowned blankly at *Eck loves Jessie*. 'No.'

When she told him he started to sweat gently and muttered, 'Jesus!'

'Are you *sure* you can't come back tomorrow?' Pamela Trevelyan pressed him artfully. Crofts could hear her breathing quite hard now, and knew she wasn't only being provocative. He began to hate Eric Harley and Harry Mearns and Scotland an' ill-met Commander bloody Simpson – no doubt thoroughly unfairly, but nevertheless Commander Edward Simpson RN retired in particular, without whom the rest could have been waging the Third World

61

War up in these God-forsaken mountains without his knowing.

'I'm sure,' he muttered sickly. 'Please believe me, Pam: if I could, then I swear I really would.'

'I do believe you, you know,' she assured him gravely. 'By the way, where are you phoning from?'

Yet another disconcerting change of tack. He relaxed. 'Auchenzie. A public call box. Can't you hear me shovelling money into the slot?'

'Whereabouts in Auchenzie?'

Crofts blinked uncertainly before screwing himself around and squinting through the grimy kiosk windows. He could see the lights of the one and only hostelry burning dimly across the narrow street.

'Opposite the local pub: The Caledonian – which sounds, incidentally, a helluva lot more grand than it looks. Why?'

'Will you phone me from the same place tomorrow, Michael?'

He frowned. It seemed an odd request, but then, on reflection, she was an irresistibly odd young lady. He decided not to push his luck. 'If you want me to. Any special time?'

'Midday.'

The time pips started to clamour again and he frantically tried to feed in another tenpenny piece. It jammed in the slot. 'Dammit!' he snarled, then the signals ceased and he knew he only had seconds left before they were cut off.

'I'll phone at noon,' he confirmed hurriedly, uncertain of his plans but aware there was no time left for debate.

'Promise?'

'Yes, I promise. On the stroke of twelve.'

'From the same place?'

'Yes, yes . . .' Jeeze, but this was bloody silly. Yet nice as well; to think the silly things did matter to her.

'I love you . . .' she called, before there was a *click* and the dialling tone came back on the empty line. He echoed, 'I love you too,' then felt a bit foolish and stepped from the kiosk and walked slowly back to the Merc.

Why on earth did she want him to phone from exactly the

same call box? And why, come to that, as early in the day as twelve noon?

It was inevitable that he should brood over the appearance on the scene of Harry Mearns as he drove slowly back to Tarvit, wincing involuntarily every time his gleaming pride and joy wallowed in a particularly treacherous pothole.

Mearns had always been like that, though; unexpectedly turning up in the interview line when the word went round that another force was being raised, usually when the other pros had assumed — maybe even hoped — that he'd finally managed to get himself killed by some ex-comrade with a long memory. Even the secret jobs, the really clandestine ones — Harry always seemed to learn about them in time to appear at whichever bar they were recruiting from, whether in London or Jo'burg or Hamburg: like the proverbial Phoenix rising from the ashes of lost campaigns.

And that wasn't an entirely fanciful thought, either. Every time CSM Mearns had been involved the job had seemed to end in disaster — the Vietnam affair f'r instance, in which Vietcong Charlie had always seemed to be one step ahead with stronger-than-anticipated security around the intended targets and their only alternatives to commit suicide or abort the mission.

And there had also been that Rhodesian frustration — when his wound had sent him out to begin his sad affair with Laura only to discover the rest of the boys shipped back to Jo'burg equally abruptly, and just as they'd really started to sort out the Terrs. That fiasco had all been because someone had indiscreetly blown the existence of a politically embarrassing international mercenary force to the world press.

And then had followed Angola. Christ, Angola! And the never resolved doubts about how the Cubans and some black SWAPO unit who'd normally have trouble planning an aggressive football match . . . how *they'd* managed to set up the ambush which had not only blown Hermann Bosche's legs away but had also crucified ninety per cent of the toughest combat column in the Africa trade.

63

But that was unfair – if you *could* be unfair about the biggest, hardest bastard you'd ever fought alongside. Because Crofts himself had been involved in all those disastrous operations, as had Eric Harley and, for that matter, poor bloody Hermann. And however much he revelled in the horror-euphoria of combat killing, Sergeant Major Mearns was still only flesh and blood. The shells which homed so precisely on Delta could have proved just as lethal to him as to any of those other retching, shock-paralysed troopers. Any soldier who invited that kind of turkey shoot with himself at the exploding end had to be completely crazy.

Crazy?

Crazy Harry Mea . . .

'Now you're the one getting bloody paranoid,' Crofts growled aloud, before glancing guiltily in the rearview mirror as if some non-existent eavesdropper might have heard him talking to himself.

But there was nothing paranoid about his suspicions of the moment. No way was Mearns employed at Tarvit in the capacity of . . . *grieve*, was it? The foreman – of a farm? Hell, Harry Mearns wouldn't know what to do with a combine harvester unless it had a grenade launcher under the seat, while his sum total of expertise in animal husbandry had been gained from sadistic drunken forays into every black bordello between North Africa and the Springbok border.

Then there was the presence of those three 'agricultural workers' Eric had allegedly hired. Admittedly Crofts hadn't met them before, and the fact that they looked sullen, moved warily, spoke Scots with excruciating Boer accents an' sported haircuts like close-trimmed nail brushes, didn't prove they weren't genuine sons of the soil. But he still laid odds on their previous field equipment having been more like general-purpose machine-guns than rural tractors.

It was all adding up to an irritating jigsaw of indeterminate shapes. Crofts glowered into the darkness as he passed the old airfield and the quarry, resolving to have things out with Eric as soon as he got back. They'd shown real concern for each other in crises past: surely to God they could talk this one out before the inevitable happened, when people like Mearns became involved, and someone – maybe even Eric himself – got killed?

He'd already decided there was no point in pressing Laura on the subject of Harry Mearns. When he finally left the Mercedes in the yard and entered the house Crofts discovered there was little point in questioning Eric Harley that evening, either.

Laura drew him hurriedly into the kitchen before he'd time to call 'Hello'.

'He's been drinking,' was her bitter greeting. 'He's been in a foul mood, Mike: particularly since you arrived. It's almost as if he's expecting something to happen tonight, but he daren't go ahead with it because you're here.'

'Tonight? Why d'you think that?'

'I heard him talking with Mearns and the others, just after you went into Auchenzie. Not clearly, but enough to sense they weren't terribly pleased. Anyway, he said they'd better go ahead without him. And then something about a . . . a "Dry gun".'

'Dry *what*?' Crofts echoed.

' "Gun", I think,' she frowned. 'I couldn't hear very well and . . .'

'I know,' he said. 'You don't like eavesdropping on Eric. Not even with the best intentions in the world.'

Her eyes filled with involuntary tears. 'I don't know what to do, Mike. He's not himself; he even seems to resent me being here. He was furious at first, when I arrived and surprised him, and even now he still keeps telling me I have to go back as soon as possible . . . but I won't, Mike. I won't leave Eric even though I know he wants me to.'

Crofts stared at her, sympathetic but at the same time relieved as one particularly worrying part of the riddle abruptly made sense. 'You mean he didn't *ask* you to come to Scotland? You just turned up uninvited on the doorstep?'

Laura sniffed an unhappy little smile. 'You make it sound awful, too. But Eric wanted to get things right here before I moved from Johannesburg: and to see the worst of the winter over. We'd planned to move in properly in the late spring, unless he decided to give up the lease and go back to Africa.'

Crofts didn't say anything because he didn't want to hurt her, but that didn't stop him putting two and two together. About Eric's non-existent preparations to make Tarvit a permanent home, for instance. Added to the discovery that, if it hadn't been for Laura's own determination, then Den of Tarvit Farm would only have had Harley, Mearns and three military-style heavies to discourage any casual local interest about what happened within its boundaries. And that Eric had seemingly been preparing the ground for his return to Africa well in advance. Before he'd ever moved into Tarvit, in fact.

At least Eric Harley *had* tried to prevent his wife from becoming involved, and for that small confirmation of their continuing love Crofts felt glad. Yet it made him more concerned as well, for if Laura had unwittingly placed herself at risk – and by her stubbornness, she undoubtedly had – then what compulsion could still be driving Eric to carry on with his operation? Why in God's name didn't he simply cut his losses, pull out and leave Mearns and Co to blow the bloody world apart while he sat in the South African sun and they both stayed poor but alive?

Or was it outside Eric Harley's control? Could Eric be under threat of death if he aborted now. Could that explain the tension that was slowly demoralising him?

Yet if that was the case – why had someone tried to kill him today. *Before* whatever was planned had been accomplished?

'Tonight, eh . . .' Crofts mused as he kissed Laura reassuringly on the cheek. 'A "*dry* gun", you said?'

'You're not going to do anything silly, Mike. Promise?'

'I might if you don't go to bed this minute,' he smiled, 'by succumbing to the temptation to drag you screaming into mine . . .'

66

After Laura had gone upstairs he found Eric in the tiny sitting room, gazing bleakly into space, a bottle beside him and far too much of the good local distillation in him already to risk upsetting that simmering alcoholic balance.

Crofts said, 'Well, is the Mess open. Are you going to offer me a dram, then?'

Harley eyed him, blearily guarded.

'Only if you don't ask bloody silly questions, ol' boy.'

'I won't,' Crofts grinned with total dishonesty, and so they sat until midnight before the wood fire, he and Eric, and drank malt whisky – Crofts very little; his host considerably more – and just for that little while rediscovered a closeness that Crofts had begun to believe was lost forever.

But eventually the heavy-lidded onslaught of the drink took its toll, and Eric Harley slumped lower and lower in his chair and became more and more maudlin. Crofts knew there was little time left for talk of any kind.

'What about Harry, Eric. Why d'you need Harry Mearns to help you on the farm?'

Eric blinked uncertainly. 'Harry? *I* don' need Harry, Mike. They're the ones need good ol' Company Sarn't Major Harry . . .'

Crofts leaned forward encouragingly. 'They? You mean the boys he has with him?'

'The boys!' Eric sneered contemptuously. 'They're rubbish, those three. Rubbish! You an' I, Mike; we wouldn't've let 'em carry our spare ammo on the job. Rubbish!'

'So who are "They"?'

Harley peered at him, trying to focus, and Crofts could suddenly see anger flickering within the befuddled eyes. 'They're the ones who think I'm Judas, Mike – that's who "They" are! They reckoned me f'r a Judas as well. Jus' like that gutless little pervert, Thomson.'

Crofts frowned. He wasn't aware of any Thomson, straight or sexually deviant, operating even on the fringes of the mercenary world. Eric continued to grumble, seemingly careless now of his presence.

'Gutless, stupid little queer. Christ but the *fish's* got more brain than Thomson, Mike boy. In fac' the fish c'n think better than any of us.'

It was Crofts' turn to blink. A shadowy, apparently somewhat bizarre Thomson – and a FISH? A fish that could *think*?

He collected his thoughts hurriedly, loath to lose the advantage while Harley was confused within his alcoholic haze. 'What about Thomson and the . . . ah . . . fish, Eric? Isn't that a pretty way-out perversion, huh?'

Harley suddenly sensed danger. His vacant expression tightened. 'What's Thomson to you? Thomson's dead!'

But then the drink finally took him and he slumped abruptly, his voice a slurred misery. 'They killed the wretched fairy, din't they? He went to see the Mermaid full of hope f'r a brave new bloody world in his corrupt little way – an the bastards mutilated him instead!'

His ramblings trailed away. Crofts sat frowning at his unconscious friend for a long and thoughtful time before he finally rolled the inert amateur farmer on to the settee and gently, even affectionately, covered him with a rug. Eric Harley would be well out of the way until morning.

He switched the light on when he went up to his room, but only briefly: for just about the length of time a man would take to prepare for bed. It didn't take him long to change into dark trousers and a black jersey, or to smear earth from a convenient pot plant as uncomfortably familiar camouflage across the highlights of his face.

After extinguishing the light and moving to the window he waited patiently. Within minutes his eyes had regained their night vision: it took only a little longer to detect a movement in the darkness followed, quite incredibly, by the flare of a cupped match as whoever was riding shotgun on the house carelessly lit a cigarette. Crofts idly speculated which of the three heavies Harry had left to keep an eye on him, and couldn't help a grim smile as he thought what CSM Mearns would have done to that useless bloody soldier if he'd known.

The cynical amusement didn't last as he left the farmhouse by a rear window; there were too many other things on his mind.

Such as a murdered homosexual called Thomson. A fish, that could 'think'. And even a *Mermaid*?

CHAPTER EIGHT

There was only one place he knew which might afford a beginning. Using the natural cover and avoiding the track itself he headed briskly seawards, keeping low, even crawling briefly as he crested the high ground between himself and the old jetty. Mearns' slapdash sentry had done rather more than simply expose himself: he'd also confirmed Laura's belief that something *was* about to happen tonight; something that Mearns seemed anxious to deter over-inquisitive house guests from participating in. Something involving a . . . dry gun?

Crofts heard the gentle growl when he was still skirting the edge of the old quarry where trapped and sullen waters mirrored the monochrome shine of that chill Highland night. There was an awesome quiet out there, the kind of silence you could almost clutch in your hand, like a soft veil whisping down from soaring mountains sharp as black paper cut-outs against the moon-bright sky.

Until the growl came. From the sea. And Crofts knew he was heading in the right direction.

He could make out the lines of the closing vessel as soon as he snaked his way to the point where Harley had parked the Rover that afternoon; on the edge of the low cliff overlooking the cove — a low, prowling craft about thirty metres long, betraying the arrogant silhouette of power. She was maybe half a mile to seaward still, and heading slowly inshore. Crofts could hear the distant grumble of idling turbo-charged engines more distinctly the moment he raised his head to clear the acoustic baffle of the land.

Frowning he watched as she came closer, slowing even

more now, pushing a vee of sparkling water to either side which spread in ever-widening ripples across the glass calm sea. Closer, ever closer to the entrance of Quarry Cove – Eric Harley's allegedly 'un-navigable' approach. Though how *was* she proposing to accomplish it? By radar? With ranges and bearings and a tight intake of breath? Crofts knew enough about pilotage to realise that any entry within such fine rock-fringed tolerances allowed little time to translate electronic images into alterations of course, and he'd already seen that no leading marks remained: beacons so placed that when aligned the entry heading was immediately evident.

Closer, and closer: the flared bow almost abreast of the jetty: gliding remorselessly through quickly dwindling water. Jesus, that skipper had to possess nerves fashioned in high-tensile wire. Still forging ahead to bring her midships section abeam of the quay-head and that intriguingly refurbished crane – only a spit left now between the bows and a shelf of inshore rock that didn't need any radar warning to send a lesser mariner screaming for his lifejacket.

Crofts tensed – there was someone running out along the irregular length of the jetty; another indistinct figure amidships on the deck, the swing of an arm as a heaving line was thrown across the narrow gap, then a heavier line snaking quaywards from the bow fairleads. He heard the gentle *clank* of metal on stone as the line was secured through one of the jetty mooring rings – those rings polished so compromisingly friction-bright – and an abrupt roar of briefly applied power while the white water threshed and creamed as rumbling screws bit astern.

She was swinging steadily now; her stern arc-ing out as she rounded the knuckle of the jetty, turning neatly against the tension of the bow spring to settle, then stop, alongside the stark skeleton of the ancient crane. Ridiculously Crofts was conscious of his own sigh of relief: even as a non-seaman he was aware he had witnessed the almost-impossible. Now, surely, he could hope to solve at least the mystery of Laura's curious 'Dry gun'.

Only he didn't. For no sooner had the dark invader

71

secured than she began to move again – away, this time: springing back around the jetty and gliding astern out to sea with that same deceptively casual expertise. Yet the disconcerted Crofts was *certain* that nothing has passed between ship and shore: no disembarking figures, no cargo, not even a package to justify the risks the anonymous vessel was taking.

And then she did it again, after she'd drawn half a mile off. Deliberately turning in a wide circle and making a second approach along precisely the same line. Slightly faster this time; the glassy sea being split rather than pushed aside; spreading astern of her in a wider, more turbulent fan of sparkling wavelets; heading on a die-straight course for the minute entrance to that impossible cleft in the rocks.

It was then that Crofts discovered how they dared to try such a hazardous manoeuvre – only a reflected glimmer from below betrayed the secret; a red glow against a shoulder of rock as if from a shaded torch. Curiously he scanned the falling ground between himself and the approaching vessel and detected a second gleam from some carefully positioned guide. Two lights shining seaward, directed by Mearns and Co no doubt: keep them accurately in line from the wheel of the closing craft and you had temporary leading night marks into the old quarry cove.

But why, dammit? Why bother to guide them in at all when they didn't *do* anything when they arrived?

Yet nevertheless she approached, and berthed; then immediately departed again! And approached, and berthed an' . . . Five times altogether they completed that pointless manoeuvre; each time a little faster; each time a little more proficiently, yet with no apparent aim at the end of it. Like a military exercise; a seemingly motiveless repetition of tactics where you stormed the enemy walls but were never allowed the satisfaction of shooting the defenders with real bullets. Just a bloody boring dry run every ti . . .

Dry gun . . .? 'Dry RUN!'

'Dry *run*' must have been the phrase Laura had misheard, dammit! That certainly described what the anonymous ship out there had been doing, in conjunction with Harry Mearns' mobile lighthouses – exercising! Reducing the risk and the time-scale in preparation for the real event.

But that, whatever it happened to be, was scheduled to take place – when?

Crofts lay waiting in the dark after the vessel had finally disappeared seawards heading south, possibly towards the Clyde. He wasn't in any doubt but it seemed prudent to confirm it was Mearns and the two remaining 'farmhands' holding the lights down there. It was. Very shortly they passed out of sight in the darkness; Harry erect as a bristle, jaunty and indestructible as ever, while his sons of the soil slouched astern, cold and tired and not the sort Crofts would have employed at all.

He waited a little longer. Mearns had learned his survival on the same harsh battlegrounds as Crofts; had adopted the cunning of the mongrel survivor. It wasn't beyond Harry to delay awhile further on, just to make sure no one was shadowing him. He began to wish he had the Beretta with him again: suddenly he felt naked without a weapon. Crofts was under no illusions about what Mearns would do to him if he discovered he'd been observed. His original determination to lead a peaceful retirement seemed a little out of place in current circumstances. Now, if the situation erupted, his immediate reaction might have to be 'Blow the bastard's head off, then make your apologies to society'!

It was not until he was about to stir himself that he heard the slightest noise from nearby. Only a rattle of stones; a handful of scree accidentally kicked over the edge of the cliff and down into Quarry Cove. He froze again instantly, hugging cover and gazing fruitlessly into the darkness. A little while later, some way away, he thought he detected another echo, but he might have been wrong.

He rolled over and lay on his back, staring up at the sky. He was in no hurry, and there was plenty of thought-provoking material anyway, to while away the small hours. Like a fish with a thinking brain, for instance: plus a mermaid? Add a mutilated corpse called Thomson; a darkened ship and a clutch of fortune-hunting mercenaries.

Top up the whole enigma with binoculars from mountain-sides and self-propelling rocks . . .

And now the intriguing revelation that someone *else* had been observing the Tarvit dry run in addition to Crofts.

He couldn't help wondering if Eric Harley *was* sleeping as soundly as your average drunk usually does.

Unless, of course, Laura happened to be an insomniac as well?

He came down late that morning. Eric greeted him sourly – convincingly hangover-sourly – but there was an element of brotherly triumph there as well. 'Some of us have been out an' about for hours, chum. The whisky up here's f'r men, not boys.'

'Shut up an' gimme some of that coffee,' Crofts muttered, looking dramatically ill. Laura came in with a basket of washing, looking even less likely to have been coast-watching all night. She smiled sweetly. 'Sleep well, Michael?'

'Like the living dead, I'd say,' Eric grinned, suddenly world's better. Then he traced a pattern on the table with his spoon and said casually, 'Did I . . . ah, say anything last night? Anything silly?'

Crofts shaded his eyes from the light. '*I* should bloody remember.'

'What do you want to do today, Michael?' Laura asked.

He jerked his head in unenthusiastic deference towards Eric. 'I did offer to be a working guest – maybe Farmer Giles here needs a hand to muck out whatever he mucks out?'

'*No!*' Harley reassured him quickly – rather too quickly. 'No, you go off an' see Scotland, Mike. Take your ostentatious machine where it rightfully belongs; on the scenic route to Loch Awe or somewhere. Don't worry about us.'

Crofts cheerfully agreed. Not only did it suit him better to be free – there were certain things he wanted to find out, and alone – but he was hardly surprised: he'd never anticipated that Eric would encourage him to wander loose on Tarvit land anyway. The relief in Eric's eyes was adequate proof of that.

'O.K.! So I'll be a tourist. D'you want a day out in a decent car, Laura?'

Her face fell. 'I can't, Mike. I'd love to, but I promised to open the craft shop for Mrs MacLaren at two o'clock. Her foot's been troubling her. She's got to go into Oban for treatment.'

He watched Eric closely, curious to test how important it really was for Harley, Mearns and the 'Boys' to be left unobserved that afternoon. 'Come to that, we could leave the run till tomorrow,' he pondered deliberately. 'Maybe I'll just wander around locally after all; breathe a bit of Highland air.'

'You can go *again* tomorrow, can't you?' Eric snapped, driven again to that strained, nervous aggression. 'What's the point in hangin' around here with nothing to do? Well, Scotland's a big enough place, Mike: you can't exactly see it all in one bloody afternoon!'

Crofts avoided the concern in Laura's embarrassed gaze, shrugging in meek compliance.

'I suppose so. Hardly likely to see much happening round Tarvit Farm. Eh, Eric?'

He parked the Mercedes near the solitary telephone kiosk and glanced at his watch – 11.25: still half an hour to pass before he bowed to Pamela Trevelyan's illogical whim and rang her as promised. If the transient vandals left the bloody thing serviceable that long.

He lit a Lucky Strike, slid a James Last cassette into the rat-trap mouth of the *Blaupunkt* stereo deck, then sat in the car gazing absently down the empty street which formed the main artery of Auchenzie village. It started to rain as Crofts wrestled with the puzzles raised by the previous night: the darkened vessel; the precisely ordered approach, the lights which almost certainly indicated that whatever was planned *was* to take place during the hours of darkness. So the next question had to be whether she proposed to land some illicit cargo – or to load it?

And how big would it be – how heavy was it? Could that,

for instance, explain the curious refurbishing of the ancient jetty-head crane?

'Ohhhh, Lord!' Crofts groaned, gripping the wheel abruptly. A distant figure had materialised at the end of the street: an unnervingly familiar bulk bearing down upon him with the rapacious determination of a killer whale in search of something to swallow.

Panic overcame him as he looked desperately for an escape route. There existed few terrors which Crofts *in extremis* couldn't face with steely jaw and English pluck, but the Scottish Mother of Auchenzie was one of them.

The welcoming refuge of The Caledonian hotel beckoned from across the road. Crofts scrambled from the car and hastened for cover, barely avoiding a secondary collision as a lorry roared within inches of his fleeing heels. It was only the shockwave of its passing that caused him once again to register white stencilled letters proclaiming *Royal Navy* to all it nearly destroyed.

'They'll be the death of some puir auld soul one o' these days,' the barman sympathised as Crofts tumbled into the deserted Tartan Lounge. 'Ah saw him fae the window. They're aye drivin' like they wis in the Monte Carlo Rally, they young Navy lads. Will it be a dram, then? Tae rebuild yer nerves?'

'Glenfiddich if you've got it – a double,' Crofts confirmed with feeling. 'They're passing through regularly then, the service trucks?'

'On their way tae Ardarroch. The trials range.'

'Trials?'

'Underwater weapons. Evaluation trials, they call them. Mines, torpedoes: onything new that needs testing has tae go to Ardarroch for the boffins tae blow things up wi' first.'

'Have one yourself,' Crofts invited. 'You seem to know a lot about the Navy.'

'Ah wis a twenty-two year man masel',' the barman said with a touch of pride. 'Finished as artificer P.O. Submarines, mostly. It's no' what it wis, the Navy.'

'What is?' Crofts agreed morosely. 'This trials range at Ardarroch. Is it far?'

'About fifteen mile north: twenty, twenty-five minutes by motor car, say.'

'All top secret stuff up there, presumably?'

The barman looked severe. 'You'll be anither Russian spy, ah suppose? We're aye gettin' them in here for a vodka on their way up.' He laughed hugely.

Crofts smiled beatifically. 'I'm undercover. I fool everybody by drinking whisky.'

'*Slainte mhath!*' the barman toasted, lifting his glass.

'Cheers!' Crofts said, and diplomatically changed the subject. But he couldn't help thinking about darkened ships again. And people who spied on other people in the middle of the night.

He had to fiddle to remove the jammed tenpenny piece of his previous evening's call before he could telephone Pam Trevelyan. It seemed no one had summoned the energy to attempt Auchenzie's solitary public link with the outside world since then. When the hotel switchboard answered he pressed a new coin in and said, 'Miss Trevelyan, please. Room Six Nine Two.'

'Connecting you, sir . . .'

The modulated London voice came back a few seconds later. 'I'm sorry, sir: Miss Trevelyan has left.'

He squinted at his watch, suddenly anxious, but it was only four minutes past noon. 'Did she leave a message to say when she'd be back?'

'Miss Trevelyan has checked out, sir. Late last night.'

Crofts gazed numbly at the kiosk's moronic defacement, not really caring whether *Celtic's the Champyons* or Ranger ever would get the heid pit richt onnem! The receiver started to scream an urgent reminder and he replaced it absently. Checked out late last night? But it was only last night she'd asked him to phone again: and right now. From this particular callbox.

Even when somebody opened the door of the kiosk he hardly noticed. His whole new world had disintegrated. Already Eric's self-inflicted bloody martyrdom had destroyed his peace of mind; now she'd gone, too. And he didn't even know where to begin searching for her.

'Are you going to occupy this box all day?' a soft but petulant female voice demanded. He stirred miserably and turned to leave.

'I'm sorr . . .'

'. . . or are you going to kiss me instead?' Pamela Trevelyan said as she threw her arms around him. Outrageously defiant. Right there in the rain-damp street of Auchenzie, Scotland.

CHAPTER NINE

Crofts pulled the Mercedes into a lay-by two miles north of the village and switched off the ignition. He'd taken one long, dismayed look at the blonde vision after he'd prised her loose; then grabbed her arm and propelled her across the pavement and into the car, ignoring her excited squeals of protest. He didn't know precisely what had caused him to react like that – he'd simply sensed, somehow, that it could prove vitally important for her own safety that nobody in the Auchenzie area knew of their connection. Or more particularly; nobody at Den of Tarvit Farm.

He turned to face her ominously. 'Phone exactly at noon, you said. From the same callbox?'

She wriggled unrepentantly like a little girl. 'It was only so's I would know where to find you. If I'd asked, then you wouldn't have let me come, would you?'

'No.'

'Anyway, you were four minutes late. Don't you love me any more?'

He glared at her. 'Don't be silly. And I was only delayed because there was money stuck in the slot . . .'

He broke off as she began to giggle. It was only then that he realised that *he* was already apologising to *her*. 'Either way, you can't stay, dammit,' he growled. 'There's no room at the farm.'

'There is at The Caledonian: lots of them. I've already booked in. Baggo's nice.'

He blinked, diverted again. 'Baggo?'

'The licensee: Mister Nialls. He was in the Navy for years and that's what they called him – Baggo Nails.'

Crofts remembered the barman who knew all about what Russian spies drank, and that made him think of sinister things. And sinister things reminded him of Harry Mearns again and why he, Crofts, had come in the first place.

'Well, you can't stay here in Auchenzie,' he said emphatically. 'And that's final.'

'Yes I can,' Pamela retorted even more positively. 'And *that's* final, too.'

Crofts blinked, muttered, 'Oh!,' and felt completely out of his depth. 'Look, I can't explain but there are reasons why you shouldn't have come here. Good ones.'

'I know that. You're in some sort of trouble, aren't you?'

He shook his head defensively. 'No, I'm not.'

'Well your friend Eric is, then. And I'd guess, with you, that's the same thing.'

'I've already told you he was.'

'I don't mean with bank managers and broken-down tractors, Michael. It's more serious than that, isn't it?'

He began to feel trapped again: she possessed an uncanny ability to sense when he was avoiding the issue. She must have guessed last night, while he was prevaricating over the telephone. For a young woman she was remarkably perceptive – or perhaps he was a very bad liar. He gave way a little further, but only because he didn't appear to have any option.

'He's got himself involved in something that might prove a bit . . . rough. I honestly don't know what, but I can't just ignore it. And anyway, there's Laura to think of.'

'Laura?'

He unzipped the bag uncertainly, disconcerted as ever jealousy, only an earnest concern. He knew he'd compromised himself beyond recovery: there was a determination in the gaze of Pamela Trevelyan which demanded nothing less than the complete truth – or *she'd* be probing around Den of Tarvit Farm next.

'It all started that morning in London,' he surrendered wearily. 'After I'd left you I really did dump the Beretta. But then I met a chap called Simpson . . .'

It took twenty minutes. He told her everything: all about

Eric and the unhappy Laura and Harry Mearns; Quarry Cove and the curious evolutions of the night before. He even related the inebriated indiscretions of Eric Harley, though with a certain reserve because it was difficult to talk seriously of thinking fish and mermaids. He actually joked a bit about them – but not when he added the reference to someone named Thomson: you couldn't make light of murder; even one included in a drunken fantasy.

Pam obviously didn't think you could, either. It was the only time she drew a sharp breath while he was telling her the story.

When he'd finished she took his hand and squeezed it gently, looking up at him with big blue eyes. 'Why don't you go to the police, Michael? Why put yourself at risk when you haven't done anything?'

'What would I tell them? Besides . . .' He hesitated: tales of mutilated dead men, no matter how fanciful, still unsettled him, 'I don't know how deeply Eric's involved yet: whether any laws have been broken. I'm damned if I'm going to risk putting him inside in the uncertain belief that it may save his life.'

'So you're going to poke about under stones instead, searching for some imagined violence to come, and be too loyal and stupid to ask anyone for help even though you might see whatever danger there is too late – and get *yourself* killed as well?'

'I might have put it a little more delicately,' he snapped tightly. 'But if that's the way you see it – Yes!'

'I thought you'd say that,' Pam said meekly. She reached behind her, hauled a British Airways travel bag over the seat and dumped it on his lap.

'That's why I brought you this. It's the most useful present I could think of under the circumstances. It's brand new, by the way, and guaranteed for twelve months.'

He unzipped the bag uncertainly, disconcerted as ever by her mercurial change of tack. It was only after he'd unwrapped the heavy parcel it contained that he received his ultimate shock.

'*Jesus!*' Crofts exploded involuntarily.

When he discovered himself holding what had to prove one of the most lethal, to say nothing of unorthodox and highly illegal, tokens of love ever offered.

. . . a Walther P1 double-action pistol. Complete with ten clips of 9 mm high-velocity ammunition.

'Where did you get this?' he ground out.

'It's only a German one,' she said apologetically. 'I couldn't find another Beretta in time.'

'*Don't* change the subject! Where did you *get* it?'

'And I only brought it because I guessed you were going to be stubborn. You've got to promise you won't actually use it unless something terrible's about to happen and you've no choi . . .'

She broke off abruptly as Crofts grabbed her by the shoulders, shaking her in blind frustration.

'Where . . . did . . . you GET IT?' he roared.

'Daddy,' she whispered in a tiny voice.

'And where did Daddy get it?'

'He . . . he's a sort of ordnance supplies contractor, Michael.'

Crofts stopped shaking her and she blinked back at him with wide-eyed innocence. God, but she could look so damn submissive when it suited her. 'Ordnance contractor? You mean your father's an *arms dealer*?'

'He's very strict about it,' she protested. 'It's all done under license, and he only deals with approved governments.'

'Unless sweet little Pam wants a gun or two to give to her casual acquaintances, of course,' he growled. 'Then Daddy just opens the lucky bag and hands out Walther P1's like jelly babies.'

'That's not true; you're hardly a casual acquaintance,' Pam pouted. 'And he has to maintain a security armoury for samples in the house. I simply . . . well, borrowed the key.'

Crofts shook his head, staring at the gun disbelievingly. 'And to think that you once asked *me* to promise I'd never done anything to put democracy at risk – while Daddy seems happy to blow up the whole bloody world f'r a profit.'

She gave him a tentative sideways glance full of devilment. 'I told you you'd get on well with Daddy.'

It was only when he began to laugh despite his determination to be angry that the full impishness of Pamela Trevelyan was finally demonstrated.

'I'd have brought you a proper machine-gun,' she frowned apologetically. 'Only I didn't think they'd let me bring it aboard the aeroplane.'

'Where are we going?' she asked a few minutes later as he drove steadily north.

'Maybe I'm heading for the nearest airport to send you straight home.'

'Seriously,' she demurred, tracing shameless, suggestive little patterns on his knee.

'To Ardarroch.'

'The Royal Navy base Baggo told you about? Why – do you think it could have anything to do with Eric Harley?'

'Probably not. But I can't think of anywhere else to start and, besides, it gives me time to think about what to do with you.'

Pam laid her head on his shoulder and squinted up through cheeky blonde strands. 'I know what you could do with me. If you stop the car.'

They drove for a little longer and some houses came into view; then a metal sign announcing *Royal Burgh of Ardarroch*. It looked nice; neat and clean and not like the industrial graveyard that had been left to smother Auchenzie.

'We're here,' Crofts said rather obviously. 'Presumably the R.N. establishment's through the village, on the other side.'

'I'm hungry,' Pamela complained. 'I haven't had anything since my plastic breakfast on the Glasgow shuttle.'

He frowned at the shop fronts as they passed through, then pulled into the kerb abruptly. 'There's a sort of teashop. At least you'll get a sandwich or something.'

They went in. The little cafe was still suffering its out-of-season quiet but an elderly lady smiled welcome from a

83

glass-fronted counter piled with cakes. Crofts ordered a coffee while Pam indicated an awesome selection of diet-contemptuous confections and asked for a large pot of tea. When their motherly hostess brought them she said, 'I've put some scones out for you, too. And a few oatcakes.'

Crofts grinned and shook his head in pointed disbelief.

The lady dismissed him cheerfully, 'Och, she's just a hungry young lass. They'll be gone before you can sneeze.'

Pamela glanced at the still-laden display. 'I might even have to help by eating some more. However do you sell them all at this time of year?'

'They'll all be away by five o'clock, don't you worry,' the matron assured her. 'I get the local farmers in on their way back fae the Oban market and they've aye got a sweet tooth. Then there's a lot of retired people who live in the big houses around; and the wives from the establishment come in about four to collect the children fae the school.'

'The Naval base, you mean?' Crofts asked quickly; it was an unexpected opportunity. 'There are families there as well, then?'

'Mostly belonging to the civilian gentlemen – aye: the scientists and such from the Ministry. Mind you, we don't see them all that often otherwise in Ardarroch. They live in the government houses down on the lochside and it's a gey long haul without a motor car.'

'You hardly notice the Navy's here then, it seems,' Pam encouraged her, seeing Crofts' interest.

'Only when they're testing; the occasional wee explosion fae the distance. Though there's the helicopters, mind; now they're awfy noisy, the helicopters that come down tae drop the experimental devices in the sea loch. And the big lorries passing through, of course.'

After she'd busied herself behind the counter again Crofts finished his coffee and glanced at his watch. It was nearly two o'clock. Restlessly he stared out of the window, waiting for Pam to finish. It had been over-optimistic, expecting to hear anything of interest from a casual conversation in a tearoom, and he had a special reason for getting back to Den of Tarvit in ample time. A quick run past the gates of R.N.

Ardarroch and they could then concentrate on more likely reasons for Eric Harley's preoccupation with the area.

They walked to the counter and asked for the bill. Crofts paid and turned towards the door while the teashop lady smiled at Pam. 'I hope you enjoy your visit. You'll be up from England, maybe?'

Pamela nodded. 'We are – from London, actually. And thank you for the scones; they were lovely. And real Scottish oatcakes make such a change.'

'One of the policemen who was here last year on the investigation said exactly the same thing. He was from London too, if I mind correctly.'

Crofts stopped abruptly. 'Policemen?'

'Och aye. There were quite a few of them here, asking questions. All strangers, they were. Not the regular gentlemen from the establishment.'

'They must have caused a stir. Was that a long time ago?'

'About last July it would have been. Aye, July: when that . . . och, it has to be said – that *odd* scientific gentleman didn't return fae his holidays abroad.'

'Odd?'

The dear lady looked severe. 'There had been complaints in the village that he spent far too much time talking to the wee boys: yon kind of behaviour's no' healthy for a grown man. But that was no call for the poor soul to have been murdered like that: and him only half way through his package tour in Scandinavia too, or so it was said.'

Crofts eyed Pamela urgently. She burrowed in her bag, playing for time. 'Before we go, can I have a quarter of those butterscotch sweets, please.'

He wandered casually back to the counter while their hostess reached for the shelf. 'This . . . ah . . . scientist: what was his name? Do you remember?'

Frowning, the lady stared at the scales. 'Thomas, was it?' She added a few more butterscotch cubes and then lifted a finger in triumph. 'Och, no, the gentleman they were enquiring about was called Mister Thomson.'

Crofts met Pam's suddenly chalk-white face with an expressionless gaze, but his mind was churning. Thomson!

The subject of Eric Harley's drunken ramblings. Thomson – the name of an allegedly mutilated homosexual who had gone to see the Mermaid, full of hope for a brave new world . . .

Just before they left, he hesitated. 'By the way: that Mister Thomson you mentioned. Whereabouts in Scandinavia was he murdered, do you know? Could it have been in Denmark, d'you think? Copenhagen, for instance?'

'Aye, I do believe it was,' the lady answered without thinking. She only began to stare after him as he gently closed the door. 'But however did you guess a thing like that?'

They came to a high wire fence about a mile the other side of the village. Almost immediately white-painted boards with red letters came into view:

MINISTRY OF DEFENCE (NAVY)
You are now entering a
RESTRICTED AREA
Unauthorised persons are
not permitted within these
grounds and are
LIABLE TO ARREST

Neither of them spoke while Crofts drove on. The significance of the unexpectedly confirmed murder of a man called Thomson hadn't escaped Pam Trevelyan any more than it had Crofts. She was pensive, as if realising for the first time that the game of love and pistols could turn sour.

As they turned a bend they came upon the gates. Red and white barriers blocked the entrance from the main road: there was a kerb of white-painted stones leading past a glass-fronted sentry box with a larger administration building just inside the wire. Another sign surmounted by a Royal Naval crest confronted all who passed by.

Ministry of Defence (Navy)
UNDERWATER WEAPONS TESTING
RANGE: R.N. ARDARROCH.
All visitors please report to
Guardroom.

No sign of other buildings was evident; even the road within the establishment disappeared into dense forest as it dropped to sea level and out of sight. There were no Naval personnel in evidence either; only an R.N. Land Rover sitting outside the guardroom and two large Ministry of Defence policemen – the 'MOD Plod' Crofts had once heard them unkindly referred to as – standing talking in the windbreak of the sentry box.

He had a feeling that R.N. Ardarroch wasn't quite as undefended as it appeared to the uneducated observer, though. It was simply the British Services' way even in these days of the possible terrorist hit: the soft-silken glove concealing a mailed and aggressive fist.

'We'll drive past, then turn and come back,' Crofts decided. 'Somehow I don't think they'll encourage undue interest, not even from someone as pretty as you.'

He found a farm track a little way on and reversed the Merc with difficulty. The main north road was as narrow here as it had been round Auchenzie – where anonymous people dropped rocks on other people in motor cars. No one dropped a rock on them at Ardarroch, however, and soon they were cruising slowly towards the gates again.

This time another car, one which must have followed them when they left the teashop, was turning into the establishment. The MOD Plod had moved forward and were inspecting papers presented by the driver. One keen glance in the back at the individual sitting there, and the sergeant waved them through to the guardroom where the first signs of the Royal Navy's presence had become evident – a Chief Petty Officer, saluting smartly and stepping forward to open the rear door as the car drew up.

'He must be important,' Pam commented, while Crofts nodded, craning his neck to see as much as possible as they continued past.

'Official car and driver at the tax-payers' expense. Very nice indee . . .'

Then he jerked upright, exclaimed, 'Jesus!', and almost continued into the verge of the oncoming bend. She squealed 'Look out, darling!' and clutched his arm in panic as he wrenched the wheel.

Checking in his mirror that they were out of sight of the gates he pulled in and switched off without a word, staring grimly ahead yet not really seeing. Pam gazed at him anxiously, unnerved by his expression.

'Michael? What's wrong, Michael?'

He muttered tightly. 'I don't know – yet.'

'But you saw something. What was it?'

He didn't move for a long time, sitting there trying to get to grips with the fast-mounting sequence of events. Finally he swung round to face her.

'You're going back to London. Tonight!' he said in a voice which even Pamela Trevelyan must have sensed brooked no argument.

Her eyes betrayed her shock: she'd been so sure he'd let her stay now his initial outrage had subsided. She was too young, too naive to accept that violence could reach out and destroy ordinary people like her just as easily as it appeared to have done with a little man on a package tour of Scandinavia

'Why?' she asked in a tentative voice.

'For one thing, I want you to talk to your Daddy: to ask him a question for me – something he might just be the best person to answer.'

'And the other thing?'

He avoided her eyes this time. 'Because I do know now that it's a damn dangerous business Eric's got himself into. And it's not one which I can avoid, either: not even if I wanted to. It seems it's been planned to involve me as well, Pam. Right from the word "Go"!'

'But how, Michael. You must have a reason. What *did* you see in that place to make you so sure, all of a sudden?'

'Oh, I've seen a reason, all right. In fact I've just seen the one and only reason – for my ever having innocently blundered up here to visit Scotland and good old Eric Harley in the first place.'

'Reason?' she whispered.

'A what I thought was a "met by sheer chance" reason a

couple of days ago.' Crofts snarled as the resentment grew fiercer within him. 'Now sitting in the back of that official car. A reason called Simpson – Commander Edward Simpson, Royal Navy, to be more precise . . .

. . . who'd *also* claimed to be retired!'

CHAPTER TEN

'I don't want to go back to London,' she said tremulously after they'd re-negotiated the pleasant main street of Ardarroch and Crofts was accelerating hard down the Auchenzie road.

'I don't *want* you to, either,' he muttered. 'But you're still going!'

'Anyway, what can you possibly want from Daddy that I can't ask for over the telephone?'

'Hopefully, highly classified defence details. And Daddy, even your Daddy, might be a little loath to contravene the Official Secrets Act twice in one conversation.'

'Twice?'

'It'll be hard enough to convince him to give you the information I need. He won't be fool enough to risk compromising his Ministry contracts by broadcasting it to you over the public telephone network.'

'What information?'

'As much as he knows about R.N. Ardarroch: particularly concerning any new weapons currently under evaluation there.'

'And what makes you so sure Daddy *will* have access to Top Secret stuff like that?'

'He's an arms dealer, isn't he?'

'An ordnance contractor,' Pam corrected primly.

'Big enough to afford a daughter who goes on shopping expeditions from five-star London hotels, and a chauffeur-driven Rolls Royce. He'll know as much about secret developments that go bang as the Prime Minister does; you bet on it.'

'It still doesn't guarantee that he'll tell me, even if he could. He'll want to know why I need the information, and I can only explain about you – which is a crazy story anyway. He's no reason to trust you, darling: not that much.'

'He will if he's the man I think he is. After you've given him his Walther back and confessed your sins in a suitably penitent manner. Wrap it up and put it back in your bag now.'

She looked at him in concern; childish resentment gone. 'But I want you to have it for protection if you won't go to the police. That's partly why I came in the first place.'

'And I'd keep it,' he said with heartfelt sincerity; thinking about Mearns again, and the awful thing that had seemingly happened in Copenhagen, 'if I didn't love you. But you've overlooked the fact that it's registered in your Dad's name. If I ever had to use it; even if the police picked me up in possession of it – he'd be finished with the armament business. And probably with you, too! I can only hope he'll appreciate my reminding you of that, and trust me a little because of it.'

'You're very clever,' she said, snuggling into his shoulder despite her disappointment. 'You've got it all worked out, haven't you?'

He had to allow himself a cynical grin as the grey chimneys of Auchenzie came into view. Mercenaries in Scotland – one of them a curiously reluctant mercenary at that? Ships in the night; an experimental weapons establishment; a dead homosexual scientist in another country. And a chance meeting in London which hadn't been chance at all.

. . . and Pamela Trevelyan thought he'd got it all worked *out*?

Christ – Crofts couldn't even begin to guess why he *himself* had been deliberately lured to Den of Tarvit Farm.

Yet!

He left her standing outside The Caledonian, gazing forlornly after him as he headed with sick heart back towards Tarvit. But he hadn't dared go in with her: Harry Mearns and the 'Boys' lived there too, and while he didn't think for one moment they would be around in the middle of this particular afternoon he was still apprehensive of advertising any link between himself and Pam Trevelyan.

'Go in and tell Baggo whatsit you have to leave suddenly: illness in the family or something. Then get a taxi back to Glasgow. You'll make the evening Heathrow shuttle . . . I'm sorry; I daren't take you. I have something else I must do.'

She'd clung to him tightly. 'There's a . . . tension in the air. It's going to happen very soon, isn't it?'

'I'll phone you for the Ardarroch information. Sometime tomorrow,' he said, trying hard to be rugged and practical if only to forestall the tears welling in her lovely blue eyes. And not succeeding.

'I'll never see you again, will I?' was the last thing she had whispered.

'Of course you will, silly,' he'd contemptuously dismissed her fears. 'They'll have to kill me before they can sto . . .'

'Dumb bastard!' Crofts exploded furiously as he spun the Mercedes into the farm turn-off – he'd been so damned intent on projecting a reassuring macho image that he hadn't even realised his getting killed was precisely what she'd meant when she'd said it.

The Merc wallowed in an unnoticed trough and he swore again. Still, he was nearly breasting the top of the high ground now, before the track fell away to the old quarry and the sea. He'd noticed yesterday, when Eric brought him back after the 'accident', that practically the whole of Tarvit Farm opened to view just at that point.

Pulling the car to the side of the track he cut the engine, glancing at his watch. It was nearly four o'clock. He'd thoughtfully bought a pair of binoculars after they'd left the teashop in Ardarroch; leaning over he withdrew them from the glove compartment then got out of the machine and walked briskly to the ridge, easing himself to the prone position before his silhouette broke skyline.

For a few minutes he saw no movement at all; just lay there minutely scanning the coastline and the deserted, gorse-infested farmland that Eric could have done so much to clear yet had apparently ignored. He began to feel a bit disappointed. Harley had seemed so anxious to steer him clear of Tarvit that afternoon that he'd felt certain something was scheduled to happen.

Pensively he lowered his binoculars and chewed his thumb, thinking about Simpson. It didn't make sense, any of it. There was no doubt in Crofts' mind now that his meeting with the bowler-hatted pirate in Selfridges had been carefully engineered. And it was too great a coincidence to believe that Simpson's interest wasn't, therefore, specifically directed towards present happenings at Den of Tarvit – for why else would the snaring of Crofts have been mounted in the first place? Most certainly Simpson had to be involved in whatever was currently taking place behind the wire fences of the Ardarroch testing grounds. So why encourage Crofts' blundering presence? Surely – if Harley and Mearns presented some as-yet unspecified threat to the Royal Navy – Simpson already had the whole of the British security forces to draw assistance from?

Christ, that was Top Secret stuff being jeopardised up there. One word to MOD and he could have had the Royal Marines, the SAS, a squadron of tanks and an airforce-full of Jaguar fighters smothering Tarvit Farm under a military cloud. So what did Simpson need *Crofts* for?

Suddenly there was a movement from the direction of the old airfield. Crofts grabbed for the glasses and levelled them in time to watch Eric Harley's Land Rover pull from behind the control tower and accelerate across country, heading for the sea and Quarry Cove. There were five men aboard; unmistakably the Tarvit hit team. There was a further, more ominous factor too: Crofts had seen too many military personnel carriers not to recognise the stiff-seated attitudes of those in the back of the Rover. They were carrying weapons. And presumably not the kind used by sporting Scottish gentry to knock down the odd pheasant either.

He watched impassively while the figures left the Rover and disappeared into Quarry Cove; one – Mearns, it seemed – remaining on guard beside the vehicle. Then they all reappeared again and clustered round the ancient gantry at the top of the cliffs – only now it seemed that, like the crane at the pierhead, the hoist had been refurbished as well.

Steadily the group hauled until a long, unidentifiable payload rose into view from below. Then, as if acting a carefully rehearsed drill, they swung it gently into the back of the Rover; climbed hurriedly aboard again, and hit the trail straight back to the airfield control tower.

Three more times they repeated the same operation: each time taking the same load back to the cove – and then returning it to the control tower, while each run took a little less time to complete. Crofts knew he'd been watching yet another rehearsal; another military-style exercise . . . and that he'd fitted one more little piece into the Auchenzie jigsaw. Whatever was to be moved was. long; probably cylindrical – and pretty damn heavy!

Like, say, a . . .

'Michael? Is that you, Mike?'

Crofts blurted 'Jeeze!' and rolled over in shock. Laura Harley was looking down at him with an uncertain, half-comical frown. His reflexes must have been dangerously out of tune to have missed her approach.

'Get down, f'r cryin' out loud.'

'Mike?'

'Get DOWN!'

She crouched, eyeing him apprehensively, but he couldn't risk them being observed right then. The Tarvit team had just left the control tower, presumably satisfied as there was no load in the back of the vehicle. He rolled over with the binoculars, just in time to watch them disappear in the direction of the farmhouse itself. It was then that the careless flash from the slopes again caught his eye.

'I was on my way home from Mrs MacLaren's. She's back from Oban: they want her to go for a minor op tomorrow instead, and I've promised to open the shop again. Eric isn't due to pick me up until six so I thought I'd walk. What were you looking at, Mike? Was it something to do with Eric?'

Crofts didn't answer for a moment, still scanning the mountain behind them. Eventually he simply nodded and said, 'Yes.'

And felt even more frustrated, because he couldn't identify the figure of whoever had, apparently, been watching *him* with as much continuing interest as he was showing in the curious goings-on of their mercenary neighbours.

They waited a few minutes. It was nearly five o'clock. Eventually he wriggled astern from the skyline, then rose and walked back to the car. Laura followed doubtfully.

'Now what, Mike?'

'I want to have a look at the old airstrip. And get the Merc off this road: if Eric's picking you up he could come this way at any time. Or even Mearns and complement, en route to their digs. Then making a detour could be more obvious.'

'I want to come with you.'

'There's no need. There's probably nothing much to see and Eric might be early – he'll wonder where you are.'

'I still want to come. I'm not prepared to bury my head in the sand any longer, Michael.'

He gazed at her pensively. There was a determination in Laura's eye which made him draw back from a refusal – apart from which, he had a nasty feeling she would shortly find her head yanked from that sand anyway, prepared or not.

'Get in,' he said. 'It's time we had a talk.'

And so they did; quietly and without histrionics as Crofts drove carefully along the rutted, weed-entangled path towards the control tower. He told her as much as he knew: even about Pamela Trevelyan and his feelings for his so-sophisticated tomboy. He'd watched Laura apprehensively from the corner of his eye while he broached that particular subject, but she'd only shown genuine delight tinged, perhaps, with a little sadness because she must have known that she and Eric had long passed the time when trust had formed part of their love too.

He didn't tell her about the unfortunate Ministry scientist, Thomson. It was the only point he avoided. But how *could* you suggest to any woman that her husband might, even indirectly, have been involved in the mutilation and murder of a man?

It was only after they'd drawn up by the derelict tower

and he'd finished his tale without a conclusion, that she said quietly, 'I think I know *when* it's going to happen, Mike. Whatever "it" is.'

Crofts stared at her. 'You know?'

'We had a dreadful row again this morning; after you'd gone. Eric pretended he wanted to surprise me – he gave me a ticket for the London train and said he'd already booked my hotel: that I could spend a few days shopping, relaxing. He even had theatre tickets arranged; everything. I told him I wouldn't go: not while you were still here. That it would be unforgivable to dismiss you like that after all these years.'

'What was his answer to that?'

'That you'll be leaving tomorrow, anyway,' she answered flatly. 'He's going to tell you again this evening: that the past is done with, and he's determined to cut loose from it. And from everyone connected with it.'

'Maybe he should've started with Harry Mearns,' Crofts muttered. 'Then I might've half-believed him.'

'I didn't even know until you told me – that Mearns had been a mercenary too. I only knew I didn't like him.'

'There's a lot of dead soldiers'd agree with *that* sentiment,' Crofts reflected savagely. But he didn't actually say it out loud. 'When has Eric booked your ticket south for.'

'Friday. The overnight sleeper from Glasgow.'

Only two days left. He stared bleakly through the windscreen, down the concrete swathe of cracked and overgrown runway. It hadn't registered with him during yesterday evening's casual exploration that its westerly heading had been laid directly towards the edge of the cliffs and out to sea, more or less passing above Quarry Cove. Like the irrevocable dive from the flight deck of a carrier . . . too damn close to abort once committed! How many pilots had sat in this precise spot moments before take-off, assessing their prospects of survival beyond the next few seconds, never mind days.

'Laura,' he frowned abruptly, 'in Scotland, in the spring; don't the shrubs usually get more green on 'em; not less?'

She blinked at him. But he'd already left the car and was crawling on his hands and knees, tugging with complete environmental disregard at the roots of the more mature saplings sprouting through the derelict landing strip of the one-time 814 Squadron, RAF Coastal Command.

'They've all been dug out,' Laura said blankly a few minutes later. 'Every decent-sized tree and bush along the runway. Dug out, then loosely replanted during the past few days.'

'And the major cracks have been in-filled,' Crofts supplemented. He allowed a handful of loose earth to fall: it was still damp. 'Probably only this afternoon by the feel of it.'

'They're expecting an aircraft, aren't they?' she hazarded.

He had to grin. Well, it was a little bit obvious, wasn't it, and anyway, she was already staring apprehensively up at the sky as if the anticipated flying machine's arrival might be imminent. 'Not right away. It'll come in at night. Low enough over the sea to avoid radar.'

'But why clear the runway, then replace everything?'

'Because it'll only take them a few minutes to open it again — and probably put the stuff back as soon as the visitor's gone. We did a lot of it in the jungle: sort of instant runway but still camouflaged ninety-nine per cent of the time.'

Laura gazed around the deserted airfield; so quiet again with only the whirr of insects and the faint cries of the gulls. She suddenly shivered. 'I came here a few times after I'd first arrived; when everything about the farm was still an exciting novelty. But I didn't like this part: it almost feels as though it's whispering with ... not-quite-ghosts, I suppose.'

'Not-quite-ghosts?'

'Of too-recent history. A dead past, but one which still isn't old enough to diffuse the fears and loves and disappointments any wartime station must have seen.'

He hesitated, surprised. 'It was forty years ago. Can ghosts really stay voluble that long?'

'*I* already existed forty years ago. As a child — we both did! Now I'm middle-aged. Perhaps this place reminds me of me; makes me too conscious of my own mortality.'

97

Crofts moved closer to her; as vitally aware of her as he'd ever been, realising that her mellowed sexuality was stirring a reaction in him that Pamela Trevelyan would never be able to match until she, too, grew very much more mature.

'You know, I've always wished you'd married me instead of that useless soldier,' he said recklessly. 'Dammit, I still do wish that, middle-aged or not!'

Laura gazed into his eyes with an exquisitely tender sadness. 'You have someone else now. And I still love Eric, Michael. Please save him.'

'Shit!' Crofts muttered, turning towards the vacantly-gaping door of the control tower. 'You're always being so bloody *practical*!'

The rusting plough was still there: the coils of old wire, the straw . . . a section of drain piping appeared to be the only recent addition to the mouldering junk within.

Crofts eyed it blankly. It was around six feet long – the height of a man – yet its circumference was such that any man hidden within would have had to be very compressed – and also, presumably, very dead! So what else might it be used for? Because that tubular mock-up certainly had to represent the object of the mercenaries' attention an hour before: the glinting scratches left by a wire sling betrayed that much.

The ends had been sealed with roughly trimmed wooden discs. Lifting one end with difficulty he hefted it thoughtfully. It was heavy; heavy enough to require, say, four men to move it any distance. As he eased it down he squinted into the gap formed between the cast iron casing and the stopper: the pipe appeared to have been weighted with ordinary, perfectly legal earth.

So it had to be merely another exercise: a makeshift prop in substitution for the real target. To be replaced eventually by, say, a canister containing some undetermined substance then . . . drugs, maybe? But if so, then why ship 'em in simply to fly 'em out – if that *was* the intention?

And then he considered RN Ardarroch again, and Simpson, and the first possibility to enter his mind when his binoculars had focussed on that elongated load rising to the top of the Quarry Cove hoist . . . and suddenly Crofts *did* know what that rusted length of piping must represent.

'I think I've got it, Laura. What the cargo might be.'

Only Laura wasn't beside him any more, she'd moved outside again; still uneasy in that dank and foetid ruin. He straightened up, dusted his hands and felt a little nearer the truth.

'Mike! Oh, God . . . MIKE!'

Her muffled squeal held the shock of terror. He whirled, sick foreboding already acrid in his throat, scrambled desperately for the door – and then halted. Framed stark against that black rectangle, a perfect target lit by the evening sun and without a hope in hell of living past another frantic step, his thirty years of battle ground survival conditioned Crofts for one reaction and one reaction only . . .

He froze. Rigid. While trying hopelessly to plan any next move at all.

There were six men altogether: all in anonymous khaki fatigues, all crudely hooded under the black woollen masks so beloved of the recognition-shy para-military animal. Three were kneeling, weapons already levelled: one Spanish Z-62 model Star submachine gun sighted between Crofts' eyes; a Czech, or maybe a Polish-manufactured machine pistol at his chest; and the last – a thoroughly unsophisticated sawn-off shotgun of indeterminate origin but which still offered the most chilling deterrent of all – trained rather more casually in his general direction . . . which was all the aiming it would bloody well need!

Two more were forcing Laura down, pinning her arms and legs, crucifying her against the concrete runway with a disciplined brutality which frightened Crofts on her behalf more than any fumbling defilement could have done.

The sixth man wasn't even sparing Crofts a glance. Slowly, deliberately, he reached behind his hip and withdrew an eight-inch hunting blade from its sheath. He knelt, unzipped Laura Harley's neat blue anorak, slid the point of the knife within the taut blouse just below the arc of the pinioned woman's rib cage.

Only then did he turn his head to stare at Crofts. His eyes were slits through the rough-cut hood; black ice-chips glinting a derisory promise. It was only as his knuckles whitened around the handle of the knife that he smiled – but it was a malicious, wool-fringed leer of awful intent.

Crofts blurted out, 'No! Oh, f'r Christ's *sake* NO!'

Laura began to writhe, whimper, struggle dementedly against the restraining hands. The Woollen Men were all grinning in anticipation now, the weapons trained on Crofts wavering fractionally, almost invitingly, as trigger fingers absorbed first pressure . . .

Crofts accepted he had no alternative but to die; heard his own bellowing hate dimly, as if filtered through the cobwebs of a nightmare. 'You BASTAAAAARDS!'

At the penultimate stroke of his reckless suicide, even as he leapt carefully forward, the knife flashed along and upwards slitting waistband, blouse, lingerie. Laura screamed, reared, the scalpel-honed edge exposing her arching cream-pale torso: stripping her without touching, yet still violating her by the utter lasciviousness of the act.

Crofts only learned there must have been *seven* hooded men when a rifle butt, swung from the blind spot on his quarter, slammed into his groin. He was still berserk, still staggering blindly forward to help her, when it hit him again.

CHAPTER ELEVEN

Crofts lay there, disciplining himself to keep his eyes tightly closed, willing the pain and the nausea to subside.

He was tormented by images of what must have happened to her; God, even as he delayed they might still be using her. But right then he couldn't detect any sound more appalling than the cries of wheeling gulls and the rhythmic hush of the sea – their prospects for survival must be marginally more favourable than he'd originally believed; otherwise he'd be dead already. Their persecutors had to be a tightly-disciplined group, professional weapon-masters every last thug. It would have taken only one untrained finger to squeeze from first trigger pressure into panic and he would have exploded like a bloodied puffball before he'd taken his second step.

Then who? And from where? Crofts had recorded a lot during those frozen initial moments framed in the door – Mearns hadn't been among them, he was sure of that, neither had any of his three recruits – so had another apparently independent force materialised to complicate the Auchenzie riddle? Crofts gave up the unproductive guessing game, and opened his eyes.

Laura was sitting watching him from a few yards away, hunched forward, the blue anorak drawn almost carelessly – as if it didn't really matter any more – across her breasts. Her gaze still held the listlessness of shock, but her concern was directed solely towards him.

They were there as well; still hooded, still observing him with the arrogant confidence of the armed superior, yet they seemed less threatening now: the weapons held more loosely, more contemptuous of any threat he might pose. Only when he attempted to move did he understand their complacence. His hands and ankles had been securely bound with rusted fencing wire.

As soon as she saw he was conscious she tried to rise, until the man Crofts presumed to be leader laid the blade of that bloody awful knife against her neck and Laura subsided with a tiny, involuntary whimper.

Crofts asked, very coolly indeed, 'What happened to you, Laura?'

Her voice was shaky but defiant. 'Nothing, Mike. They haven't touched me.'

He leaned back against the wall of the control tower and closed his eyes again, aware only of an overpowering relief – and an even greater confusion.

A kick snapped his eyes open again. He found himself staring furiously up at the man with the knife. The eyes within the black slits returned his glare imperturbably.

'The woman has a good body, Crofts. It would not be too difficult to encourage my friends to . . . enjoy her further discomfort.'

So they knew his name. But the impersonal reference to 'the woman' – were they unaware that she was Eric Harley's wife? Crofts fought to clamp his rage under tight control: you didn't lose your temper with a chilling bastard like that. Not more than once, anyway. And he needed to listen; to try and learn as much as he could. For instance the man spoke with an . . . American accent, was it? Yet there was something else there, too; a faltering precision, as if English was a not-entirely familiar tongue.

'You've presented the argument,' he muttered. 'Now relay the message!'

The wool-shrouded lips eased fractionally, but there was no humour there. 'The message reads: "You will leave Auchenzie, Crofts . . ."' There it was again – that elusive, vaguely European inflection. The *ch* of Auchenzie pronounced as a hard *k* . . . 'To be even more specific, you are to leave Scotland altogether. You will go quietly and without attracting attention . . .'

'Why the hell should I?'

'Are you really so anxious to learn what we could do to your woman?' the Leader asked almost indifferently. He raised his leather-gloved hand and immediately two of the men dragged Laura down, pinned her arms again. She screamed, heaved convulsively as a third knelt above her.

'*No!*' Crofts bellowed. 'I'm listening, dammit!'

The Leader shrugged, dropped his arm and they roughly released her. She began to sob while Crofts felt himself shaking uncontrollably – but he'd also learned a little more. When the Leader had raised his arm Crofts had noticed an unmistakable, blue-white scar briefly exposed above the black glove; the kind of scar which only chemically-burned flesh bore for a lifetime. Crofts had seen such scar tissues often: in Vietnam – particularly on the Communist side of the Demilitarised Zone after a U.S.A.F. napalm strike.

'You are reckless with her well-being, Crofts. You will ensure that you have left by this time tomorrow afternoon. Furthermore, you will tell the man, Harley, nothing of what has happened. Neither will you refer to this incident or to the existence of my group to anyone at any future time. Do you read me loud and clear now, Crofts? Without any room for misunderstandings?'

Crofts said, 'Yes!' It was surprisingly easy: as if his hate made the lie so much more pleasurable.

'Good,' the Leader nodded. 'Because, should you choose to disregard this warning, then wherever you hide we shall find you both again. But next time, after my companions have finished, the woman will only survive as meat, Crofts: violated and mindless meat – while you will simply be an unrecognisable corpse.'

Laura was fantastic. Oh, she'd cried after the Woollen Men had melted away and while she was struggling to release the wire around his wrists. She'd even clung to Crofts at first as he massaged his circulation back and swore with black frustration, but eventually she'd sniffed, and looked remarkably brave as she tugged and tied and tucked her defiled clothing around her; and finally looked at her watch.

And squealed, 'It's nearly half past six. Eric will be worried about us,' as if that was the most serious thing to happen that day.

He ground to a halt, suddenly conscious of his own lack of consideration. 'Are you sure you're all right? Not too upset to go home yet?'

She dropped her eyes but her voice was steady. 'I'm humiliated; I'm embarrassed; I feel dirty and I've been more terrified than I'd ever have believed possible – but I can't afford the luxury of hysteria, Mike. That creature said Eric hasn't got to learn what they did to me – to us – and he's not going to, not from me.'

'Oh, bugger Eric!' Crofts flared passionately. 'It's time he did face up to the truth: what it's doing to you.'

'*No!*' Laura blurted out with an intensity that frightened him, underlining more than any tears just how close she was to breaking point.

'. . . No, Mike,' she continued more levelly. 'I want you to leave here tomorrow and forget about us. Whatever Eric's doing, he's doing for me: I've got to believe that for my own sanity, don't you understand?'

'All right,' he nodded with a bland acquiescence which, if she hadn't already been so uptight, would have worried her sick anyway. 'Then I keep quiet: I even leave tomorrow – but only on one condition.'

'Condition?'

'That you do what Eric wants, and get out of Auchenzie as well. Travel down to London – and then we're *all* bloody happy!'

She gave him a thoroughly miserable look. 'Happy?'

'At least you'll be well clear of those evil bastards with the nasty minds,' Crofts comforted.

Though he didn't really believe *that* statement himself.

At least Eric wasn't waiting when they got back to the farmhouse. Laura even managed to bathe and change and appear looking fresh and composed before he did return; betraying few outward traces of her traumatic assault.

It all began to go horribly wrong from then on, though;

even before they sat down to their delayed evening meal. Eric was already in a filthy mood after his wild goose chase to collect Laura: inevitably his foul temper exploded Crofts' own already-fragile tolerance. Grimly he attempted to explain that he'd met her by chance instead, and had suggested a short run before preparing the meal.

'. . . an' why not, Mister Agriculture? She works like a kaffir, dawn 'til dusk, while you're too bloody preoccupied with your own troubles to care one way or the other!'

'So what does *that* mean?' Eric flared. 'You back on that bogeymen-in-the-closet thing again, are you? Because if you are, then go back to bloody London an' write me a letter.'

'I'm bloody GOING!' Crofts bellowed back. 'First thing tomorrow morning. Friend!'

Eric had stared at him then: his anger deflated. 'Oh?' he'd said. And looked half relieved yet, at the same time, rather lost. Like a little boy who'd suddenly found himself alone with the ball in the middle of his first rugger game for the school.

'It's Mike's last evening – let's all go out tonight,' Laura said quickly, with a fragile brightness bordering dangerously on the verge of hysteria. 'Even if it's only for a drink at The Caledonian. Please, Eric.'

Which, Crofts could see, really meant: 'Let's all go out because if we sit here and hate each other any longer I'll break down'.

He glanced at his watch before he preceded them from the farmhouse. Nearly nine p.m. How cold and dark the night had become as they climbed into the Tarvit Rover in strained silence.

And how Eric Harley's features, lit by the green glow from the dashboard as he leaned forward to press the starter, adopted – just for one fleeting moment – the ghastly complexion of dead man's flesh.

The lounge bar of The Caledonian was surprisingly busy: presumably the lieges of the Burgh of Auchenzie found little else to fulfil their social needs on a chill spring evening.

Their host, Baggo – Nialls, wasn't it – was there dispensing a comforting range of spirituous liquor to those still thirsty, and good-natured counsel to those few who had already slaked their needs too well. Crofts cringed as he caught the militant eye of the Ferocious Mother gimlet-fixed in his direction through an otherwise affable crowd. She was clutching a Bacardi and Coke like a hand-grenade in purse-lipped defiance of the financial limitations placed upon her by the Department of Social Security, while wedging an understandably gloom-cast and shrivelled male into a corner. Crofts presumed with heartfelt sympathy that the imprisoned man must be poacher husband Tam; lately threatened by a Tarvit shotgun – an experience which, nevertheless, might well have proved considerably less wearing than this jolly night out with his wife.

This time the Mother chose to ignore him as he slunk past in the wake of Eric and Laura. Crofts' gratitude for such a deliverance was only diminished after they'd all sat down and he glanced towards the bar – to meet, instead, the unblinking gaze of Harry Mearns.

Oh, there was nothing sinister about Harry's presence in The Caledonian on that particular evening. Nor that of his three companions lounging, pints in hand, eyeing the Harley party with the perfectly proper respect of farm hands meeting their employers in sociable proximity. After all, they *did* live there.

But it was still strange; the sensation which came over Crofts in that momentary meeting. He'd never spoken to the ex-CSM since that brief word on his arrival – had never seen him again other than at a distance and covertly. Had he done so it could only have been a bitter confrontation – Mearns had a resentment of Crofts founded on his hatred for any authority, even that of a mercenary command; Crofts had a counter-balancing distaste for Mearns which his Angolan rescue had done little to dispel.

Yet it was in that moment when his eyes met Mearns', that Crofts understood they had very little time left. Until then it had been only a presentiment; the merest sense of events inexorably building towards a climax. Now there was an additional factor; an unmistakable message betrayed by Harry's gaze: a kind of pleasurable but tightly-bottled anticipation. It was the look, Crofts remembered, which had been the trade mark of Company Sergeant Major Mearns immediately prior to every attack Column Delta had ever launched.

Maybe Eric had seen and read and understood it as well, and become conscience-pricked because of it. Whatever the reason, he began to drink heavily once more, brusquely rebuffing Laura's tentative cautions; his glazed expression of the previous night rapidly returning, adopting the same haunted vacancy.

By ten o'clock he was black-introverted: three whiskies later his mind again lost control of tongue and discretion.

It was inevitable. The explosion was bound to follow.

Mearns unintentionally provided the flash-point. Maybe it was the way he and his troopers couldn't avoid the occasional glance towards the Harleys. Certainly there was no intention on their part to cause trouble, but Eric didn't need a reason, not any longer. He'd been staring through his glass towards the four for some time before he frowned.

'Harry's watching again,' he suddenly muttered. Before they could prevent him he'd risen and was waving an uncertain hand. 'Aw, c'mon, Harry! Come an' tell us why you're always watching, Harry.'

Laura looked at Crofts with dismay. Already some of the crowd were turning, smiling uncertainly, attracted by the disturbance.

'D'you see Harry, Mike?' Eric leered unsteadily. 'Good ol' Sarn't Major Harry?'

'Siddown, Eric,' Crofts growled. This was neither the time nor the place for a confrontation. Harley ignored him, glaring now across the crowd towards Mearns, all pretence gone.

'C'mon then, Harry, an' tell us. Or would you like me to, eh? Would you like *me* to tell 'em you're watching because you hate us?'

Crofts tensed. Mearns was moving now, smiling amiably,

but still coming over while the other three hovered uncertainly at the bar. It didn't stop Eric, though. He'd already swung round carelessly, calling to Crofts.

'They do, y'know: Harry an' the ones like Harry – they all hate us. They even hate us when they use us. We're expendable, Mickey boy. All the little men with ideals. But of course *Harry* knows all about the little guys, Harry does. They go to see the Mermaid – an' find *Harry's* pals there instead . . .!'

Mearns seemingly tripped as he came up to them; cannoning violently into Eric, interrupting the flow of garbled invective, sending a chair skittering into a corner. 'Lord, I'm sorry, Mister Harley,' Mearns said with embarrassed concern, pulling him upright, straightening his rumpled jacket. 'Me an' my feet: plain bloody careless. Look, a drink, eh? Drinks for yourself an' Mrs Harley an' your other gentleman.'

Only Crofts got the real message. Snarled in a cold undertone.

'Get this loose-mouthed bastard out've here, Major. Now! Or so help me he's a dead man . . . an' you better believe it!'

There wasn't time for debate. Nor would it have been exactly politic to succumb to his initial temptation – to lash out at Mearns, boys or no boys. Already they'd become the centre of attention in The Caledonian; everybody was staring in furtive curiosity. Baggo Nialls had moved from behind the bar and was hovering uncertainly – Laura had abruptly gone as white as a ghost.

Urgently he took Harley's arm. 'C'mon, Eric. Time to go. Give me the keys of the Rov . . .'

But Eric whirled, pushing him away, mouth working with rage. 'You? You're no better than him, you double-dealin' bastard! You an' her, Crofts: that slut wife of mine . . .'

Laura cried in horror, 'Eric! No, darling . . . Please!'

Crofts felt shame-sick, guilt-sick – apprehension-sick.

'Look, Eric, we'll talk tomorrow. Before I go.'

'To wait for her! You think I don' see it, Crofts? I don't *know* you're planning to meet up so's you c'n screw her like you did in Jo'burg — that blatant bloody *whore* hiding behind you!'

Harley lunged, striking blindly at Laura. Someone in the watching crowd screamed as she stood motionless, allowing the blow to land. Only the flowering white impact on her cheekbone and the glint of free-flowing tears marked her misery.

'Leave her alone!' Crofts roared, snatching Harley's arm, the fury in him suddenly exploding. But Eric bawled a hysterical, 'I'll bloody kill the bitch!' and lunged again. One glimpse of Mearns — even Mearns looked thoroughly disconcerted now — and Crofts had grabbed Harley, swung him round, catapulted him helter-skelter through the scattering citizens of Auchenzie and was following, impelled now by his own blind resentment.

'NOOOOOO!' Laura screamed, in such agony that every last soul in the room stilled: Crofts, Eric Harley — even Baggo Nialls in his determined aim to instil order.

Only then did Eric emit a funny gasping cry and turn; fleeing blindly from himself and the horror of what he'd done. They stared in shocked embarrassment as he lurched towards the door, until Crofts, ashen-faced himself now and suddenly frightened for his friend, called 'I'll get him . . .' in reassurance to Laura before following into the night.

Even as he raced down the steps of The Caledonian hotel he heard the diesel clatter of an engine starting up, then the crunch of tyres spinning on gravel. Eric's Rover reversed erratically from the park, collided with the front wing of a nearby vehicle, grated into first gear and finally accelerated crazily down the road towards Ardarroch, and Den of Tarvit Farm.

Crofts hesitated only momentarily: his concern for Eric outweighing even his anxiety over the appalling position they'd left Laura in. If he went back for her, even more time would be wasted, and he'd read the haunted stare on his friend's face too clearly in those few frozen seconds before Eric's hysterical flight to risk even a moment's delay. He'd only looked upon an expression quite like that once before in his life.

It had betrayed itself in the eyes of Troop Sergeant Bosche over a year before. During the moments in which he'd gazed into a nine millimetre barrel and seen therein the image of his own death.

Crofts began to run. Conscious only of a terrible fear.

It took twenty lung-tortured minutes, but he was still fit enough to cover that dark track to Tarvit without halting, driven as he was by his sense of bleak foreboding. The lights were on in the house as he came into the yard where the Land Rover sat angled and abandoned beside the quiet gleam of Crofts' own Mercedes.

The front door of the farmhouse stood wide open. Crofts halted, listened uncertainly . . . there hung a silence over Tarvit as heavy as a black velvet shroud. Some sense cautioned him to approach more slowly; easing through the door into the empty kitchen. He hesitated again: a strip of light shone from under the closed door of the comfortable lounge where he and Eric had sat the night before. Tentatively he turned the handle, eased the door a crack – then swung it open.

Eric Harley stared sightlessly up at the low beamed ceiling. He was lying on his back, arms and legs spread wide, a starfish cadaver grounded in a pool of blood. There were three, maybe four bullet holes in the front of his shirt, placed immaculately above the heart in a two-inch group. Judging by the volume of blood they had been large-calibre rounds; evacuating through monstrous but mercifully hidden exits in his back.

Whoever had killed him had done a superlative job. Eric must have presented a moving target. He was almost certainly dead after the first hit, hurled backwards by the impact and falling – yet they'd followed him all the way down, still firing; a text book demonstration of murderous professionalism.

Except for one inexcusable, curiously inconsistent error.

It seemed they had left the means of Eric Harley's dying.

Crofts registered the gun lying almost at his feet as if through a dream. No warning altered his shock-dulled mind as he knelt slowly, dazedly; lifted it without taking his eyes from Harley's body. Not even when the weapon held such strange familiarity with his hand.

When realisation did eventually dawn it was hardly necessary to glance at it to be sure. But he still did, and thus confirmed that it looked precisely as it had done two days before; prior to his scattering its dismembered parts throughout the streets of London's Soho.

Only it would appear that it hadn't really been neutralised at all – Crofts' discarded tool from his mercenary trade. Because now it had been reassembled again. Then cleaned, reloaded, and even more recently – fired.

The pistol he'd once known as Beretta M951.

CHAPTER TWELVE

Crofts was still kneeling when he heard the car draw up outside, the door slam; the urgent steps. He was still holding the Beretta and trying desperately to understand when the policeman came into the room behind him.

He was a constable, only a youngster, a schoolboy almost, wide-eyed and frowning from under a chequered cap band. He was staring more at the gun than at Eric, and he looked frightened.

Crofts became aware of a strange calm; a resignation. He felt a terrible sadness for Laura, yet only a detached and almost cynical acceptance of his own perilous position. He rose and gestured with the Beretta; offering it. 'Go on, take it. I . . . it was lying beside him.'

The policeman swallowed. 'I'm no' supposed to touch it, really. Maybe you'll place it on the table – Please sir.'

Crofts moved over and laid the pistol down gently. The constable slid quickly between him and it and then ran out of ideas. He didn't chance upon a gunshot corpse and a likely murderer in Auchenzie every day. Crofts gestured towards the former. 'Hadn't you better call for assistance? There's a telephone in the hall.'

'Is he dead then?' the boy asked, beginning to look dangerously pale at all the blood.

'Yes.'

The policeman took his hat off and hesitated, running his finger inside the band as if it was too tight. Crofts could see he was beginning to sweat with the nausea of it. 'Go on,' he urged. 'I won't run away. I'll come out of the room with you if you like, then you'll be sure.'

They went into the little hall and the policeman telephoned.

Crofts held the chequered cap with the brand new shiny
badge for him after that. While he was being sick.

A uniformed sergeant arrived within ten minutes. He
brought two more constables in a white police Land Rover
and, while one of them stayed with Crofts in the hallway,
the sergeant took the young officer outside and spoke in
tones too low for Crofts to hear.

Two plain clothes officers came next and the whole group
spent a few minutes more in conversation before, finally,
they entered. The bigger of the two detectives went straight
through to the lounge while the other glanced in, turned and
nodded to Crofts. Curtly.

'C.I.D. Detective Inspector Duncan: the one gone in there
is D. S. Reekie. You are?'

'Crofts. Michael Crofts.'

'Live here?'

'On holiday. Mister and Mrs Harley are friends.'

'Mister Harley . . . would he be the deceased?'

'Yes.'

'Andy.'

The uniformed sergeant came in from the yard. 'Aye?'

'Take Mister Crofts and sit with him in your motor.
When the doctor and forensic arrive, see they come straight
in. Is the young lad all right now?'

'It's his first. He's fine.'

'Where's Mrs Harley?' Crofts interrupted. 'Has she been
sent for?'

Duncan eyed him. He didn't appear very friendly, or even
concerned about Laura. 'She's being looked after. There's a
policewoman with her back at The Caledonian.'

Crofts couldn't help himself. 'Christ, that's her *husband*
through there! She'd want to be here, man. Not sitting in a
bloody hotel!'

The Detective Inspector gave him a bleak stare. He
seemed almost as angry as Crofts, but it was a detached,
professional anger; an unsettling contempt.

'Maybe Mrs Harley's pleased herself too much already. Maybe if she hadn't – then we wouldnae be here at all.'

Crofts sensed then that he was in terrible trouble. But he'd guessed that much from the minute he'd renewed his acquaintance with a very old and very familiar companion of battle.

Funny. He wasn't quite sure in that bitter moment of whether he was reflecting upon Beretta M951 . . . or Commander Edward Simpson, Royal Navy.

Retired?

'Tell me, Mister Crofts,' Detective Inspector Duncan said with a not-entirely-subtle offhandedness, 'have you ever seen this gun before? This Beretta.'

They'd covered Eric with a green plastic sheet after the doctor completed his preliminary examination. Crofts was glad of that; it had seemed wrong, somehow, to leave him lying there in crucified indignity. Only battlefields offered the excuse if not the justification for treating a human being's remains with contempt. He remembered one particular corpse many years before – in Cambodia it had been: some already-sickly child culled by a howitzer splinter from the endless refugee column streaming past their amtrack laager. None of the soldiers, none of the gooks had bothered to move the tiny husk and at first the incoming drivers had avoided it, but then some sweating trooper had got careless or sleepy or plain bloody indifferent, and not quite missed the corpse; and then the next in line had tracked a bit further over it . . . and then the next until, eventually, nobody even tried to divert. And in an short time the dead child had spread like a hedgehog on an autoroute to become paste while finally even the paste had been erased by the rattling amtracs . . .

. . . so Crofts was glad of the green sheet over Eric. It made it seem as if he still meant something; commanded some respect.

The police had placed the Beretta in a clear plastic bag; a little bit like they'd treated Eric Harley. He gazed at it expressionlessly. 'I've seen a lot of guns, Inspector. It's difficult to give you a categoric "no".'

'Or, maybe, a categoric "yes", eh?'

Crofts shrugged. 'I was a soldier. Soldiers tend to handle quite a few weapons.'

'British Army, presumably?'

'I . . . began there. Commissioned into the Para's.'

Duncan eyed him pensively for a long moment, then referred to a notebook. 'Does something called *Column Delta* strike a wee chord with you, Mister Crofts?'

He read the flicker in Crofts' gaze and smiled sourly. 'We have a very efficient computer link to Central Records. We also hae a wee organisation called "Special Branch" . . . and there is a telephone here, in the hallway.'

'I presume you know I was a military freelance, then?'

'Both you and the deceased, according to my information. Mind you, I aye thought you lads called yourselves mercenaries wi'out the fancy title. Though 'freelance' has a more respectable ring to it, I grant you.'

'I didn't kill Eric Harley,' Crofts said.

'You were holding that gun when the young lad surprised you.'

'He didn't surprise me! Or only because he came in the first place. How did he know?'

'The Licensee of The Caledonian Hotel reported a breach of the peace. By the time Constable Cliesh arrived you'd left – in pursuit of Mister Harley.'

' "In pursuit"?' Crofts queried bitterly. 'The way you say that speaks volumes, man.'

'Talking about things said: what did you mean exactly when you shouted to Mrs Harley as you left The Caledonian. I quote from witnesses – ". . . I'll *get* him!" was the expression. Would you accept that, Mister Crofts?'

'Christ, *I* don't know,' Crofts flared. 'I was angry . . . upset. So was Eric . . .'

He broke off abruptly. They were watching him now: all the police officers and even the doctor. 'Look: why *would* I want to kill Harley, Inspector. We'd argued before; Jesus, every friend argues with another and we'd been friends for years: we'd fought beside each other for years. We'd shared for bloody years.'

'So I gathered,' Duncan said in a funny voice. Crofts blinked at him.

'An' what does *that* mean?'

'Mrs Laura Harley. Have you been sharing her for years too, Mister Crofts?'

Then Crofts understood. They thought this had all occurred because of Laura; even when they'd first arrived: the tight expressions of contempt; the unspoken disapproval. They'd already taken statements from witnesses at The Caledonian; Nialls, the Ferocious Mother – everyone there had heard Eric openly accuse him of having an affair with Laura. An open and shut case; a crime of passion, the eternal triangle ending in post-alcoholic death.

Eric had even been killed with *his* gun! It wouldn't be too difficult for the Crown prosecution to link him with Beretta M951: he'd carried the same weapon for years; Special Branch obviously held his profile in detail, they probably even recorded the brand of cigarettes he smoked.

It was the perfect frame-up. He'd been set-up for this with cold deliberation – even helped them by offering himself as a target, dammit! They, whoever 'They' were, must have been delighted at the way he'd walked straight into a murder charge. The ingredients had been so skilfully brought together – Eric; Laura; Michael Crofts, paramour extraordinary – all it had needed then was the time and the place . . . and one highly able assassin waiting at Tarvit for the inevitable to happen.

But who? Not Mearns – Harry and his team were still at The Caledonian when he'd left to follow Eric, while nobody had passed him en route.

The Woollen Heads then? Or Simpson? Certainly Simpson had been responsible for his coming to Tarvit. Though why in God's name should Simpson want to frame him for Eric Harley's murder?

'*Michael Crofts: I am arresting you on suspicion of the wilful murder of Eric Harley. You will accompany my officers to Police Headquarters in Oban where you may be charged with such offence after further enquiries have been made.'*

Presumably Simpson had also arranged for Beretta M951's resurrection. That young couple on the motorcycle? He should have been on his guard then; even as he'd sensed he was being followed through Soho.

It was at that moment that Mike Crofts began to perceive, however late, the true depths of the intrigue into which he had so naively blundered. For if Commander Edward Simpson – an ostensibly-retired officer of Her Britannic Majesty's Royal Navy – really had connived, not only at the premeditated murder of Eric Harley but also the involvement of Crofts, all as part of some monstrous, possibly even government-approved plan then yet another question raised its head.

. . . on behalf of *which* government might that self-same Simpson RN have arranged it in the first place?

They'd handcuffed his hands before him to take him out to the white Police Land Rover. The uniformed sergeant had grasped his arm and, with Detective Inspector Duncan following, was leading him to where the young constable was already waiting, a bit uncomfortably, by the driver's door. The lad still looked pale and tired; he would have a lot more work to do.

There were quite a number of ogling locals, mostly from The Caledonian, standing behind the gate, where another constable good-naturedly restrained them. It was then that Crofts remembered the one thing that might help.

He halted abruptly: so abruptly that D.I. Duncan nearly cannoned into him. The sergeant gripped his arm more warily, firmly urging him forward.

Crofts blurted out, 'The rock! Yesterday evening. Somebody had already tried to kill Eric *before* tonight!'

'Just get into the vehicle, sir,' the sergeant insisted majestically. 'You'll no' be wanting a scene here in front of all those nosey people. There'll be plenty of time to make your statement down in Oban.'

'But the Rover's *there*, dammit!' Crofts persisted, holding his ground. 'You'll see the windscreen's gone.'

Duncan came round and frowned at him. 'Hold it, Andy. Now, Crofts: what are you claiming about yesterday evening and Mister Harley?'

So Crofts told him in a low voice: all about Eric and the levitating rock, and the unlikely accident; and he knew he'd earned a second chance because Duncan was a good police officer and could see immediately that there was a big difference between a drunken homicide over a woman and a premeditated intention to kill.

They walked over to Eric's old Land Rover under the prying gaze of the Auchenzie public. Crofts pointed with both hands. 'See? The windscreen's missing. Surely it proves *something* violent happened to Harley recently.'

Duncan eyed him. 'Even if it does, you could still have thrown it.'

'That would have been premeditation. Your theory about fighting over Mrs Harley after a drunken row in a pub wouldn't hold water, then. And if you demolish one reason for suspicion, you've at least got to re-examine all the others.'

'Did you keep the rock, Crofts? Could you even find it again? Forensic might support some of your claim.'

'Harley threw it away,' Crofts said weakly. 'Into the stream.'

'Ahhhh,' Detective Inspector Duncan nodded. Knowingly.

The uniformed Sergeant Andy suddenly leaned into the back of the Rover and hauled something into view. It was a pheasant. A dead and rather mutilated one. They all stared at it blankly until, caught in its mangled feathers, they saw the twinkles of broken glass catching the blue flashing lights on the Police cars.

'It'd no' be the first time,' the sergeant observed dryly, 'that a motor's had its screen smashed in by a bird. They fly better than granite boulders.'

'Get in the fucking motor, Crofts,' Detective Inspector Duncan said.

Wearily.

It was a dark night. They'd driven for maybe ten or fifteen minutes with the young constable uncomfortably silent behind the wheel and uniformed Sergeant Andy-something holding the plastic bag containing Beretta M951 – Crown prosecution exhibit Number One – while sitting opposite Crofts in the back of the jolting Land Rover, bleakly indifferent to his handcuffed prisoner. He'd seen them all before; all the wee hard yobbos fae Glasgow and the local farm lads wi' too much of the drink in them and stupid violent because of it; maybe he'd even met the more sophisticated ones like Crofts already, who came north from England with a misplaced contempt for Scots Law and a wee bit gun in their pockets.

Crofts ignored them both, staring fixedly through the windscreen at the rock faces flashing past lit by the headlights, and at the odd glimpse of cliff edge and black sea as they skirted the coastal road to Oban. God, it was desolate up on this western fringe of Scotland, but he didn't exactly view it with a tourist eye: he was thinking of Laura most of the time – of her sadness and of the stigma that would mark her now until the end of her days as the libidinous widow who'd sparked off the murder of her man.

He thought of lovely Pamela, too; mercifully away to London to try and learn the answers to this afternoon's most pressing riddles which had now been so horrifyingly downgraded. He had lost her now, and might never know the secret until whatever was planned, happened – and then it would be too late! It *was* too late already; Eric was dead and he was facing a possible life sentence because the police were satisfied with their evidence and wouldn't investigate further; particularly now his protestations over the shattered windscreen had further branded him a liar.

Which, come to that, raised the spectre of who had framed him for that.

'Sergeant!' the young constable called suddenly, leaning forward and peering ahead. 'There's a lad by the verge. Could be he's had an accident.'

There was, too. A figure distant in the beam of the lights; leaning weakly against a boulder and holding his arm as if in pain. The police vehicle was already slowing before the sergeant grumbled, 'Aye, well we're no' staying unless there's serious injury. They'll just hae to wait on traffic patrol after we've radioed for assistance.'

The lonely man didn't stir, even as the Rover drew up beside him; he just leant there with bowed head, a drabness of misery in his washed-out ex-army fatigues and his curiously fashioned black woollen ha . . .

'Drive on!' Crofts bellowed frantically, galvanised into desperate urgency. 'Don't stop, man. Keep her *moving*!'

But it was far too late for warnings, or for prisoners to suggest what police escorts should do, when the barrels of a sawn-off shotgun rammed through the open driver's window and ground viciously into the young constable's throat while, simultaneously, two straddle-legged figures appeared at the tailgate of the Land Rover, levelling a Spanish Z-62 and a Czech – or maybe it was a Polish submachine gun at its other occupants. Crofts still wasn't one hundred per cent certain – about the origin of that second automatic weapon.

No more than he'd been earlier that same day: the first time it had been sighted on his chest. Back at the old airfield on Den of Tarvit Farm.

CHAPTER THIRTEEN

They were efficient; horribly efficient. Every last detail of that hijack operation had been planned in advance. The only orders given were to the occupants of the Rover; Scarred-Hand never uttered one syllable to his own team.

He stepped between the gunmen at the tailgate and gestured to Crofts. 'Get out!'

Crofts did as he was told, stumbling as he climbed over the board without the aid of his free arms. The Leader steadied him roughly and Crofts jumped down. He didn't say anything: he knew nothing could be said that would matter.

'You will hand over the key for the handcuffs, Sergeant,' Scarred-Hand stated flatly. The big policeman sat tight and stared back, more outraged than nervous, for it really was an outrageous situation he was called upon to accept – that a Strathclyde Constabulary vehicle was being waylaid on the public highway of mainland Britain by heavily-armed men.

Particularly *his* vehicle!

'Och, away and dinnae be stupid, lad,' the sergeant growled uncertainly.

'The keys. Now.'

One of the gun barrels rose pointedly, lined on the sergeant's forehead. Even then he couldn't fully accept what was taking place; incredulity was still acting as a bolster to his courage.

'I'm warning you now: there's serious charges already mounting against you: you're no' helping yourselves any by further aiding and abetting the escape of a prisoner fae custod . . .'

'*Sergeannnnnnt!*'

The young constable's plea, when it came, was delivered in a shriek of agony. Crofts couldn't see what they were doing to the boy in the driving seat, but he didn't need to. 'Do it!' he shouted, 'Give him the bloody key, man!'

The sergeant could see though. He muttered a choked 'Jesus!' and began to fumble with the button of his pocket, suddenly white as the sense of outrage gave way to shock. Seizing the key without a word Scarred-Hand unlocked Crofts' handcuffs. Simultaneously another member of the ambush party stepped forward and presented his arms, wrists together. It was like watching a well-rehearsed stage performance.

The leader snapped the chromed manacles on his own man and then helped him climb over the tailgate and into the Rover. Nothing else happened; the hooded man simply moved into Crofts' original seat and stared impassively at the police sergeant opposite.

'Now you have a prisoner again,' Scarred-Hand announced humorously, still with that vaguely alien inflection. 'We take one; we give you one back, don't you see?'

Nobody laughed. In fact nobody even smiled.

'You cannae *do* that . . .' the sergeant blurted, thoroughly nonplussed. Then broke off, shying nervously as Scarred-Hand abruptly leaned into the back of the Rover, neatly whisking the uniform cap from his head. Quite deliberately the Leader then dropped it on the floor between the two seated men.

'I suggest that you pick it up again, Sergeant,' he invited, 'before it becomes damaged.'

Crofts tensed, began to move forward until the muzzle of the Z-62 ground into the base of his spine and he halted again. He didn't think he was going to be able to help Police Sergeant Andy Something-or-other very much anyway.

The sergeant went red with pent-up fury. 'You go tae hell!'

The young constable in the front immediately began whimpering again. There was certainly no humour now. 'Pick it up!' Scarred-Hand snapped grimly.

'All right!' the sergeant shouted. 'Leave the laddie be, will you . . .' He stared at Crofts for a moment; eyes bleak as granite. 'I had you placed from the start as being the richt man tae have killed Harley, you bastard: now I ken you were!'

Resentfully he leaned forward, reaching for the cap.

That was the moment that the handcuffed man sitting opposite moved too; swiftly bringing his linked wrists up and into the bending policeman's throat; a fleshly, chain-locked garrotte. There was a disbelieving half-scream, choked short as the attacker turned and twisted all at the same time whereupon Crofts saw the sergeant's polished boots drumming frantically against the tailgate of the vehicle. The handcuffed man jerked viciously, grunted: the boots rattled a final frenetic tattoo and then relaxed abruptly.

Crofts knew the sergeant was dead and felt stunned; nauseated. Oh, he'd seen and heard men die in a similar manner before, but never with such seemingly pointless deliberation: previously it had always been as a tactical prelude to battle; a sentry surprised, an enemy overcome as a necessary first move in a war in which all participants accepted the rules . . . but this wasn't a *battlefield* f'r Christ's sake. This was rural Scotland. And these men weren't fighting a war.

Or *were* they?

The young constable menaced by the twelve-bore understood that the sergeant was dead, too. Even as the passenger door was wrenched open and clutching hands reached in, holding him brutally against the back of the seat, he was crying with the terrible dawning of what was about to take place next.

It didn't take very long. Already the hooded assailant was moving from the upended corpse, settling over the second pinioned officer. This time the arms looped over, hand-cuffed wrists crossed, the right hand palm outwards and placed against the back of the head while the sharp blade of the left forearm drew hard across the struggling boy's larynx. Crofts shouted 'Jesus, NO!'

The expertly-placed right palm rammed the vulnerable chin forward, downward, levering irresistibly against the bony fulcrum of the forearm. Crofts actually heard the constable's neck snap, amputating the strangled pleas in mid-nightmare.

Impassively, almost matter-of-factly, the virtuoso in eye to eye murder released the corpse, pushing it forward against the wheel, and then clambered out to where Scarred-Hand removed the cuffs, tossing them on to the sergeant's body sprawled in the back of the vehicle. The muzzle of the gun still pressed hard against Crofts' spine, even though it was no longer necessary. Nothing could be done – nothing *had* been done to prevent the inexplicable killings, God forgive him. He felt no gratitude that, for some obscure reason, they didn't propose his own elimination. He would already have been the third of three corpses by then had they intended such an outcome.

It was Scarred-Hand who faced him; the only wool assassin with a tongue. While his combat team fanned out and watched the silent road, and Crofts prayed desperately that no unsuspecting Highland travellers would chance upon that stage of death to surely meet their own, the Leader's words were clipped, concise – and somewhat thought-provoking.

'You disobeyed me, Crofts: I ordered you to leave this area quietly . . . and yet you recklessly ignore my warning. You even kill the man, Harley, in your drunken stupidity.'

Crofts stared coldly into the mask before him, covering his surprise. So Scarred-Hand also assumed that he'd murdered Eric! But in that case, where *did* they fit into the pattern: for if they were remotely connected with any other suspect, then surely they would have guessed the truth?

The black-woollen man asked unexpectedly, 'Tell me, Crofts: are you a good soldier?'

Crofts shrugged indifferently. There was no apprehension within him now, simply hate.

'Good enough.'

The man gestured and immediately the submachine gun

withdrew from Crofts' spine. 'I hope so. You will require all your fieldcraft and military ingenuity to avoid capture. Use them well, Crofts: you may even be able to leave this country if you can reach your mercenary contacts. I suggest you begin running immediately – before the authorities discover your latest atrocity.'

This time Crofts couldn't conceal his reaction. '*My* atrocity?'

The mouth smiled faintly, a slit within a slit seen faintly through the darkness. 'Two more murders, Crofts. Both executed by an expert in combat killing – as I'm sure you are. Both committed while wearing the handcuffs you originally wore; both perpetrated from the rear of the vehicle in which you were held prisoner.'

'You bastard,' Crofts ground deliberately. 'Ohhhh, you calculating bastard!'

'A triple-murderer at large in Scotland, Crofts. And two of your victims unarmed police officers.'

Scarred-Hand began to back away. Crofts didn't move; there were too many weapons still levelled at him as the group melted into the darkness.

'The British public have a fierce affection for their policemen, and those same police are obsessed by an undeviating determination to avenge their own.'

There were no Woollen Men, no living forms to be seen now: only that aggravatingly-foreign voice was left, hanging in disembodied mockery like the smile of the Cheshire Cat in *Alice*.

'It appears that you have suddenly become a fugitive of the most hated kind, Crofts. So run, my friend, and keep on running. Surely – this time – even you will not be reckless enough to remain in Scotland.'

He worked quickly, urgently, after they had gone. There was no revulsion in him; simply simmering rage at what they had done, and at what they were forcing *him* to do.

First he searched through the rear of the police Land Rover; expressionlessly moving the bulk of a dead Sergeant Andy-something or other until, trapped below the body, he found the plastic bag containing the Beretta, unnoticed by Scarred-Hand and his team.

The part-discharged clip of Parabellum ammo was contained with it: four rounds left . . . he knew only too well where the other four were. He did hesitate briefly before smacking the clip home in the weapon receiver – each of the remaining bullets had a crossed notch cut into their snub noses: a dum-dum shell which would expand and fragment as it hit; tear the guts out've any poo . . . Crofts' jaw was set in concrete as he climbed from the Rover and moved to the driver's door.

He prayed hard in that moment. He hadn't prayed for anything apart from Troop Sergeant Bosche's eternal peace since he was a small child, but this was a very special prayer; entirely different. That he might be allowed to use one bullet – only one, Lord; that's all he asked – on the bastard who'd shot Eric.

The young constable slumped where he had been killed; head lolling hideously forward against the wheel. It fell to one side again as he pushed the neatly uniformed body over; like a turnip on a too-weak spring. The boy's diced uniform cap lay beside him. Crofts had a feeling that he must have been very proud of that cap. Gently he placed it across the poor agonised features and climbed in, reaching for the starter.

It only took moments to draw the vehicle forward on to the verge until the front wheels were poised above a gentle slope ending in the black silhouettes of gorse below. It would give him a little more time – they'd find it when they searched the road after dawn – but he needed time to get away and to do certain things to certain people.

Cutting the engine he slid out and released the handbrake again, pushing with his shoulder. The white vehicle with the two dead police officers rolled and bumped until he heard the crash of snapping branches. He peered at his watch; it was nearly four o'clock in the morning.

Crofts kept Beretta M951 in his hand as he began to walk along the dark road, ready to jump to cover should anybody pass. The gun felt good again; a welcome companion. There was no guilt in Crofts now; not over the promise to Pamela which he intended to break, nor Eric's death nor even Laura's agony of widowhood: only a desire for revenge which spurred him on.

But it did seem an odd thing for a fugitive from a triple murder to be doing when logic – even that offered by a hooded man with somewhat obscure motives – advised him against such foolishness.

. . . to be heading directly north, towards Auchenzie, when his only hope of escape lay in precisely the opposite direction: London and the southern ports. And particularly in clearing the immediate area before the alarm was raised, and road blocks made flight an impossibility.

CHAPTER FOURTEEN

The cruising white light etched every tree stark against the night. Crofts flattened himself against the ground and waited until the slowly moving police car had passed, then rose to his feet and continued towards Auchenzie. It was four-thirty a.m.; they hadn't taken long to start the search. From that moment he could consider himself elevated from the role of prime suspect in a little local murder to that of being the most wanted killer in Scotland.

As he finally skirted Den of Tarvit he saw the flashing blue lights in the distance – the police were still there, searching more determinedly along the track the Land Rover had taken before it vanished. There were lights on in the little Auchenzie police station too; with patrol cars drawn up outside and dark figures crowding the charge room. Crofts passed easily by through the shadows; he was a professional in the art of clandestine movement and besides, who would have expected to find him there? Any rational fugitive strove to open a gap between himself and his pursuers; he didn't calmly approach the hunters' base.

The Caledonian hotel, like the rest of the village, was in darkness now: the good residents of Auchenzie attempting to enjoy what little opportunity for sleep remained after the excitements of public disorder and murder most foul. It wasn't difficult to enter through a rear window and find the reception desk. Crofts examined the guest register in the dim glow from the outside street lamps . . . *Room 3: Mister Mulders; Room 4: Mister van der Spuy; Room 5: Mister Kruger* – all very exotic for simple Scottish farm lads, but perfectly legal nonetheless . . . and then *Room 6. Ah, Mister H. Mearns*!

Silently Crofts moved along the dark corridor, hesitating briefly at the creak of ancient boards; cocking the Beretta warily as Mister Mulders in room number three turned and yawned on the opposite side of his door. Gently he eased the handle of number six and slid within . . .

. . . and growled a silent oath. The bed was empty – Harry Mearns was not at home.

But Mister – or should it be *Meinheer* Mulders? – undoubtedly was. Crofts swallowed his disappointment at missing the opportunity of a chat with Harry and went back to Mulders' room instead, wherein he forced the muzzle of the Beretta straight between Mulders' strong white teeth as he lay snoring gently, and then said nicely, 'Hello, Mulders. You let out one syllable, an' I'll blow your fucking brains clear into your fucking chamber pot!'

For Crofts was weary of being a gentleman by then; and he knew precisely how to communicate with a reluctant host like Mister Mulders.

The eyes were like ping pong balls staring up through the darkness. Mulders didn't move an eyebrow, just lay there rigid with the barrel of the heavy calibre automatic swallowed in his black straggly beard, and waited for Crofts' advice on how to survive for the next sixty-odd seconds.

Crofts slowly withdrew the Beretta; confident that they had established a useful working *rapport*. Simultaneously he became aware, to his discomfort, that room number three held all the olfactory appeal of a grave-robber's armpit – Mister Mulders could hardly have claimed to have been the most hygienic of men. Crofts backed away and raised the window before returning to the bed.

'Sit up, *Springbokdung*,' he suggested. 'Place your hands on your head like the top of your skull was about to lift off an' hit the ceiling – which it may very well be about to do. Then tell me quickly where good old Harry is.'

'The farm,' the unfortunate man stammered, struggling upright and clamping his hands firmly above his head. 'The police called for him: requesting him back at Tarvit as he is the grieve . . . the foreman, *ja*?'

'I *know* what a grieve is, *dumkopf*!' Crofts snapped

shamelessly. 'O.K., so now you've volunteered to tell me things instead. First – who blew away Eric Harley?'

There was a start of geniune surprise in Mulders' expression. He didn't need to answer: Crofts already guessed that Mulders – and presumably Harry too, in that case – believed that *he* had killed his friend.

'Break to Question Two, Mulders – the operation you're setting up at the farm. What's the target?'

The Boer swallowed. 'They will kill me if I tell.'

'No they won't,' Crofts assured him earnestly, 'because you will be totally dead already, friend. I will have pre-empted them – in roughly ten seconds from now!'

'Guns! We are planning to run guns to the Irish Republicans . . .'

Crofts pistol-whipped Mulders viciously, slamming him sideways across the bed, then clutching his beard and yanking him erect again, coldly indifferent to the blood from Mulders' split cheek oozing over his hand. He placed the muzzle of the Beretta brutally under the whimpering man's chin. Even the whimpering stopped.

'Negative your last message. Say again, Mulders.'

'Hijack,' the agonised lips wavered. 'It's a hijack contract, Mister Crofts.'

'Hi-jacking what? Ocean-going drainpipes with that midnight navy of yours?'

'What do you know of *Marauder*?' the unhappy man pleaded.

Crofts shrugged. 'Nothing – yet! Except you've just given me her name. Now we'll really try hard to save your life, Springbok: next you will tell me *what* you intend to hijack.'

'I . . . I can tell you noth . . .'

Crofts prepared the Beretta for a second roundhouse swing and the bearded Boer jerked away in terror, spraying blood.

'They call it "Spearfish" . . . *Spearfish!*'

Crofts hesitated, eyeing him assessingly. Spearfish? Certainly it had the ring of truth to it: 'Fish's brains' . . . Spearfish. Allied with the RN Ardarroch connection and a length of drainage piping which, for exercise purposes, might very well represent, say, a . . . torpedo? Possibly an experimental torpedo? More than likely, a Top Secret experimental torpedo.

But did *that* suggest that Mearns, Mulders and Co had to be involved in some form of espionage; working for some enemy power, probably from the Eastern Bloc?

'Who are "They", Mulders?' Crofts asked, emphasising every word. 'Who's paying you?'

But he knew he was losing Mulders: the man was too scared of 'Them'; and while Crofts in his present mood would have been quite prepared to blow his brains out, it did promise to be noisy, too noisy for a quiet little Scottish village bulging with angry policemen.

He still tried, though: settling himself comfortably on the bed and slowly, sadistically, tracing the bloodied split in Mulders' face until the muzzle of Beretta M951 froze precisely on a level with Mulders' staring right eye.

'I have already taken up first pressure on this trigger, Mulders,' Crofts whispered, 'and I can feel myself getting very tense. I shall get very much more tense if you do not answer instantly. Now, Mulders: who . . . is . . . employing . . . you . . . to . . . heist Spearfish?'

'I tell you nothing more . . .' the man called Mulders croaked.

And whatever else the Boer had said that night, Crofts suddenly felt sure that he could believe that last tormented promise . . .

Because abruptly there came a sort of dull, slicing thud, whereupon the terrified man beside him jerked monstrously and clutched at his shoulder: blood gouted from Mulders' suddenly gaping mouth and vomited down his black, already-soiled beard – and Crofts knew beyond any doubt that Mister Mulders of room number three in The Caledonian hotel, Auchenzie, really wouldn't tell anybody anything ever again.

He was already pressed flat against the wall, the gun covering the mocking, vacant window which he himself had opened earlier, before Harry Mearns' man finally slumped sideways on the bed and Crofts registered the throwing knife protruding from his side. It was then it also occurred to him, rather too late, that his own fingerprints were now liberally represented at the scene of yet another murder.

Which meant that now he was primary suspect for *four* horrific killings instead of only three.

. . . an' he hadn't bloody well done *any* of them!

CHAPTER FIFTEEN

Crofts was foundering in limbo, drowning in a sea of ignorance.

Four men had died within hours; the first three – Harley and the police officers – unquestionably eliminated in such a manner as to point all suspicion towards him . . . and furthermore, it appeared that two separate and independently-operating hit teams were at work.

The fourth cadaver currently debited against him was at least a little different. Mulders, presumably, had been spiked with the refreshingly straightforward intention of silencing him. But who *had* knifed the unhappy Boer? Had that also been done by Eric's killer, or had it been the work of Scarred-Hand and his Woollen Heads – or perpetrated by some as-yet-unsuspected third, fourth, fifth individual, party, regiment or whole bloody army? Crofts was uncomfortably aware that he didn't even know how many people, or groups, proposed to blow away how many *other* people. Or groups.

Therefore Intelligence must become the priority for his survival – Intelligence as defined in military terms: 'The gathering and analysis of information regarding the enemy'. However Intelligence gathering demanded some facility for communication, while 'communication', in Auchenzie terms, was strictly limited to a graffiti-camouflaged public telephone box in full view of a Strathclyde Constabulary incident HQ: complicated still further by the need for a pocketful of suitable coins of the Realm.

Crofts frowned as he slipped through the open window, leaving the body of Boer Mulders to be discovered on The

Caledonian's awakening. He couldn't risk staying, in case that event took place very shortly, but also he couldn't help wondering whether Laura was still sobbing out her lonely misery in one of those silent hotel rooms. Or had she already returned to Tarvit? Might Inspector Duncan even have taken her away for further questioning, now that the whereabouts of her fugitive lover had assumed such grim significance?

The overriding need for Intelligence again. He had to establish some temporary refuge from which to think, to make contact . . . to unravel the threads. But where? Where might he be reasonably secure, yet still able to reach a telephone?

Then, just as he was skirting the shadows opposite the little village police station, it occurred to him that he might know of such a place. It promised to be unattended at least for that day, it almost certainly possessed a private phone, and it was the last location in Scotland where the police would think of searching for their most desperately wanted man.

Situated, as it was, virtually next door to their own incident centre.

The *Auchenzie Tweed and Scottish Crafts Shop* was warm, comfortable, and did indeed boast a telephone. Crofts was inordinately grateful to his unwitting hostess, the Mistress MacLaren who – according to the dimly remembered remarks of Laura the previous afternoon – was scheduled for treatment at Oban's hospital for the whole of that forthcoming day. Poor Laura couldn't stand in for her as promised; not now. It was a chance no exhausted fugitive could ignore.

A very ordinary lock, a darkened side door and his *American Express* card: it hardly called for sophisticated cracksmanship but Crofts, briefly released from the pressures of pursuit, still felt childishly elated. He might even had made a good professional burglar, he reflected – though that, mind you, would have meant going a bit down-market after being a quadruple murderer.

He moved cautiously through the blackness between racks of kilts and shelves of Highland souvenirs. There was even a little back room without windows which Mrs MacLaren used as an office and store. Crofts closed the internal door, switched on the light, and made a cup of tea with the conveniently provided electric kettle and teapot. There was no milk but he didn't mind that: he laid Beretta M951 beside him on the neatly arranged desk instead. It provided a much greater source of comfort.

First he selected a piece of Mrs MacLaren's pretty pink notepaper and wrote three names on it:

Simpson
Scarred-Hand
Mearns

He frowned at the paper and then added a fourth name, with a hesitant question mark:

Pamela?

His frown deepened to one of grim contempt for his own suspicions. But Crofts was fighting for his life now; and trust had died when four dum-dum rounds blasted the life out of Eric Harley. He added one more name – a fifth name – to the list:

Laura.

Unconsciously his hand found, and began to fondle, the gun beside him as he settled back and stared at the pink list. Unless there were further unknown participants in the Auchenzie affair, then somewhere in that column had to lie the name of Eric's killer, or at least of the individual who had contrived his murder. Crofts knuckled his forehead viciously. He couldn't ignore any possibility now. Why shouldn't it be Pamela Trevelyan? Hadn't he simply assumed that Pam had returned to London? Just as he'd assumed, until then, that Laura Harley really *was* a grieving widow.

Ohhh, Crofts really began to hate himself then. There had only ever been four people in the world to whom he would have entrusted his life. Two were dead: Eric Harley and Troop Sergeant Bosche; both ironically by the same gun – *his* gun. The other two were still alive.

And he loved them both . . .

Yet no matter how selfishly he'd yearned for the affections of those two women, he had still entered their names on a list. And it was more than a simple list of suspects to Crofts: it was also a declaration of intent.

You see: whoever was finally proved guilty; man or beloved woman – he fully intended to kill them.

It was almost seven a.m. He had to grasp the nettle firmly, whatever the result. In the case of Pamela Trevelyan there was an additional and less worthy motive for haste – even for the early risers newspapers were only then being delivered; radios crackling to life. It was unlikely at this time of the morning that she would have chanced to hear news of the Auchenzie slaughter.

And he needed to learn about Mulders' Spearfish: what form of weapon it really was; how vital its security was to the national interest. Perhaps even more importantly – the details of its current Ardarroch trials programme, so that he could estimate where and how the hijack might take place.

It was a long wait after he had dialled her London number. He found himself praying again: that she *would* be there, which would prove that she, at least, couldn't have pulled the trigger which blew Eric out of this life.

She answered herself. A little uncertainly: almost as if she hadn't wanted to. He was frowning even before he spoke.

'Pamela?'

'Michael! Oh, Michael.'

He said, 'There isn't much time. Please Pam: trust me and don't believe anything you may hear.'

Her voice was strained. Urgent. 'I do believe you, Michael. But you mustn't say anything!'

There was a crackling of static on the line and Crofts felt the hair rising at the nape of his neck. Then her voice again: breathlessly. 'They're already here, Michael – the police! Someone saw me with you in Auchenzie yesterday; your Ferocious Mother woman. They traced my address from the hotel register.'

More static and the smothered fuzzle of her receiver being

grasped. A male tone in the background, angry. 'Miss Trevelyan: you were warned not to . . .'

'Leave her alone: she knows nothing!' Crofts shouted. 'There's nothing she *can* know, dammit!'

'Michael, they're tracing this call! Oh God, I love you, darling: I LOVE youuuuuu . . .'

Crofts slammed the telephone down and found himself shaking with rage. Staring at the opposite wall he began to swear, silently at first and then with increasing feeling. The bastards! The absolute bastards! Abruptly he snatched the telephone directory and thumbed through the pages, reaching for the dial again.

This time the voice that answered was male, cool and distantly efficient.

'Navy Ardarroch.'

Crofts said flatly, 'Commander Simpson, please. Commander Edward Simpson.'

'One moment, sir.'

There was a click and Crofts waited, tracing his finger absently along the barrel of the Beretta, thinking about Pamela and hating himself for his earlier mistrust. But he couldn't deny it had existed: that fact would always be there between them.

The detached voice came back. 'Would you please give your name, sir?'

Crofts hesitated momentarily, then shrugged. Simpson would know soon enough anyway. He snapped, 'Crofts . . . Major Crofts.'

This time the delay was at the Navy end, a startled silence, then the operator coughed. 'We have no Commander Simpson here, sir. There is no record of any officer by that name in the establishment.'

Crofts stared flintily at the wall. 'I want to speak to Commander Simpson, mister. Now put me through!'

'I'm sorry but I can only repeat – we *have* no Commander Simpson, sir. Or any other rank by that name. Perhaps if you would tell me where you are I can . . .!'

The alarm bells were ringing far too stridently to be ignored. Crofts slammed the phone down, breaking any trace on that line too, and sat for a long time with the piece of pink paper before him, getting more and more frustrated.

Then he got up and laid enough tartan motoring rugs on the floor of the little store room to make a pillow, and placed Beretta M951 beside them; switching the light off before stretching out with a grateful sigh.

Crofts was a seasoned campaigner as well as a thwarted Intelligence officer. His only lines of communication had been blocked, therefore he would make use of the delay as any good soldier should. There was little more he could hope to do until darkness fell again that evening.

It was still only the eleventh hour; not the twelfth. It would be Friday night at the earliest – to judge by the surprise holiday Eric had proposed for Laura – before any Spearfish operation could have been scheduled to take place. And this was still only Thursday morning.

But try as he would to sleep, for once in his life he found it impossible to discipline his mind. Something still didn't add up; something about the Auchenzie affair which made a crazy nightmare even crazier.

All right, then – so analyse Spearfish itself . . . He knew enough now to guess that it was some form of Top Secret weapon which could actually 'think' – which unquestionably placed it a generation in advance of any underwater or, for that matter, any surface-to-air missile guidance system in current use. And which, by definition, offered a prize any Iron Curtain power would go to infinite lengths to win for itself. Spearfish, if he was on the right track, could present the espionage coup of the decade.

He began to feel even more out of his depth. Espionage! A game for specialist players, not ordinary mercenaries. A spider-game between super-powers.

. . . and that was when Crofts jerked upright again: dammit, why should he assume that this *was* some form of espionage operation? The very nature of espionage was that of the night scavenger, which crept and stole and slunk away without trace: it was a subtle, unheralded discipline in which success was to obtain your enemies' secrets without ever letting them discover that you had. *That* was the supreme art of armaments espionage. Then you could employ that secret knowledge to produce a defensive counter-weapon without forcing your enemy, once more, to devise a counter-weapon to counter *your* counter-weapon . . .

So what the hell was happening around Auchenzie, where various parties were being blown away with all the finesse shown at the battle of the Somme? Assuming for the moment that the Soviets were involved, where was their alleged sophistication? They made their espionage advances by blackmail and electronic ears an' dissemination of false information and coercion and . . . well, whatever methods the KGB used, they certainly didn't include hiring a mob of clapped-out mercenaries to heist a Top Secret bloody weapon.

Crofts lay back again in mounting frustration. He closed his eyes and tried to forget solving the insoluble; concentrating instead on all the *good* things which had happened to him since he'd first met the now seemingly non-existent Commander Simpson RN.

They didn't take long. He was sound asleep within sixty seconds.

He awoke after what seemed only moments. Bells were clamouring from the distance: short, urgent rings, the strident alarm of a fast moving police patrol vehicle. Then came the screech of brakes and the clatter of running feet from further long the street. Crofts lay for a few minutes with his hand on the gun but nothing happened: no interest was shown in his own refuge. He rolled over and went back to sleep – obviously they'd discovered Boer Mulders.

His world was still pitch black when he next awoke; this time with a start, eyes wide and every sense a prickling warning. He was on his feet with Beretta M951 at the ready before he realised that it was after eleven in the morning and it was only dark because he was in a light-proof room.

Then he heard the nearby sounds again. From the outer shop itself. Someone moving around, making no attempt at secrecy . . . yet if the Mistress MacLaren really had attended Oban's hospital for the day, then who might be out there?

By the time the storeroom door began to open and the first slash of daylight illuminated racks of plaid and short-bread moulds bearing *Greetings fae Auchenzie* and bug-eyed ceramic mini-Scotsmen Crofts was waiting, pressed flat-aback against the wall, one hand on the light switch and the gun a hovering promise.

And then the door swung wide. Crofts slid behind the incoming silhouette, slammed the door shut again, hit the switch and ground the muzzle of the Beretta into the startled newcomer's spine.

Her face was white with shock as she half-turned. He registered the glint of barely-dried tears in suddenly terrified eyes, and the reddened lids from her weeping emphasised by the glare of the store room lamps.

Crofts lowered the gun, and said helplessly, 'Laura? Jesus but I'm so sorry, Laura . . .'

They clung to each other for a long time, neither of them saying anything: each drawing desperately-needed comfort from the other. And in that time of precious interdepend-ence Crofts learned that his blackest suspicions had proved without foundation. Unquestionably he was holding the sadness of widowhood in his arms; fresh tears proving that she had no part in Eric's death.

And more. For clutched in that embrace, Crofts made a second, almost equally priceless discovery — that she assumed his own innocence with equal conviction. And for that, Crofts offered up his third prayer of the night, but this time one of thanksgiving rather than of hate.

'Why?' he asked. 'What made you come here this morn-ing? After . . . everything that's happened.'

She looked at him and said simply, 'What else would I do? I couldn't face the farm right away, and The Caledonian's alive with policemen.'

'Mulders?'

'You know?'

He nodded grimly. 'I know! Not who did it, but I do know he's dead.'

'And I've no friends, no real friends in Scotland. I just

hoped keeping occupied in the shop would help me as much as it helps Mrs MacLaren. She's a widow too, and alone.'

Crofts took her hand and she didn't resist. She didn't respond this time, either. 'You never need to feel you're alone, Laura,' he said softly.

She began to sob gently again and he hated himself: he hadn't meant it the way it had sounded; the inference it contained . . . or had he? Embarrassed he made her a cup of tea; opening the door of his self-inflicted prison a crack while he waited for the kettle to boil, and watching the street through the little shop window. Auchenzie seemed quiet enough now; no undue police presence at least within the limited sphere of his vision.

He was about to close the door again when he heard a familiar growl. A blue and white police Panda drove slowly past, followed by an Ikon gold Mercedes. There was a uniformed constable behind the wheel of the Merc too: it was his own car. That incident, trivial by comparison with what had already taken place, nevertheless emphasised Crofts' alienation from the official world. His eyes grew even harder as he turned away.

There was only one cup. They shared it and tried bravely to talk about the future until they both conceded there *was* very little future to talk about so long as the mystery of Eric's death remained unresolved.

In fact, the more Crofts listened the less sanguine he became. In low tones she told of how Inspector Duncan had been correct yet coldly remote in his unspoken condemnation of her part in the tragedy. The police were convinced that Crofts had murdered their colleagues in a successful escape attempt. It would also be reasonable to assume, by now, that Duncan believed he'd killed Mulders too. Whatever Crofts' motive, forensic must have already proved he'd been present in Mulders' room when the Boer died.

Crofts' resentment boiled over.

'But when you told them about my real reasons for coming up here: about everything we've discovered so far in connection with Ardarroch – didn't Duncan believe *any* of it? Enough to raise at least some faint doubt in my favour?'

He broke off, aware that Laura was returning his gaze expressionlessly. Rather too expressionlessly. It was that absence of feeling in her stare which caused him to hesitate; chilled him with a new and unexpected unease.

'I don't know, Mike – I didn't tell him.' she replied.

He forced a disbelieving smile, but the smile soon faded to leave only the disbelief. 'You didn't even tell . . . Christ, Laura, what are you trying to say?'

'I'm saying that I intended Duncan to assume you murdered Eric and all the others – particularly the others. Your being there when they were killed was quite useful.'

She was returning his stare now, without the slightest trace of shame. 'You see, Mike: I *wanted* to convince the police that you're nothing more than an immoral, cold-blooded killer. Without any conscience at all.'

CHAPTER SIXTEEN

Crofts found himself staring at Laura in a state bordering on shock as his hurt welled to the surface.

'Has it occurred to you that, even if you didn't give a damn about clearing me, the truth could at least have pointed the police towards Eric's real killers.'

'Or it might have helped protect them, Mike,' she retorted, still with that air of quiet calculation. 'And I want them found and punished. More than anything else in the world.'

There it was again: that unsettling malice. But at least it seemed that her hatred wasn't directed towards him: he appeared to have been its victim rather than its cause.

'Maybe you'd better explain,' he muttered finally. 'How my being on the run can help catch someone the police don't even know about yet because you haven't mentioned them.'

Her eyes were softer now. 'I was there, remember? Being questioned by Inspector Duncan about your likely next moves. And I read enough into his thinking to know he's convinced you're already heading south. They'll search the immediate area for you today – and then most of the extra police involved in your manhunt will be withdrawn.'

Crofts couldn't help himself. 'That makes me feel a *lot* better,' he growled. 'Still a four-time loser, but I'll be able to go for a stroll without quite so much risk!'

'Don't be silly!' Laura snapped with a flash of her old spirit. 'It means that Auchenzie will be quiet again by tomorrow night. If I'd given Duncan reason to believe some wider national security issue was involved, then Tarvit Farm would have been saturated with . . . oh, secret service or MI5 or whatever they are, for weeks.'

Still ruffled, Crofts nevertheless began to understand. Even if Laura *had* told Duncan of the Woollen Men and the darkened ship and the airfield and Quarry Cove it wouldn't have proved anything: it was still merely a fanciful story. Mearns certainly wouldn't confirm it: Woollen Men didn't exist without woollen hoods to compromise them. And while the security people *were* trying to prove it – asking too many questions, watching too many places – then whoever was behind the Spearfish heist would be forced to abort the operation: probably to withdraw their team – or teams. Which, in turn, could mean that whoever killed Eric might go to ground permanently.

'It's your . . . our best chance, Mike.' Laura emphasised. 'To ensure that whatever Eric was involved in continues – and that means you have to stay a fugitive for a little while longer. I'm sorry.'

He placed his hands on her shoulders and looked full into her eyes. What he had to say was going to be hard.

'You do know that the action Eric was training for – the hijack – was almost certainly going to harm this country, don't you? To be blunt – that he and Mearns were planning treason?'

'No, Mike. Please,' she said tremulously. But he had to finish.

'He was about to help steal a British secret weapon, Laura: Mulders confirmed that much. He called it Spearfish. If Eric was involved, then he simply *had* to be working for the Soviets. It's the only way it makes sense.'

'What are you trying to suggest?' she whispered.

'I've no claim to be considered a dedicated Brit: I turned my back on Queen and Country far too long ago. But I'm no traitor either, no more than you are. If we do wait, and don't even attempt to alert the security people, then we have to be damn sure Mearns and whoever else is working for the Reds can't outmanoeuvre us and get away with Spearfish. Establishing my innocence, even finding Eric's killer, doesn't justify an irresponsible gamble. We've still got to provide a backup in case the worst happens – and to do that, we've got to trust *somebody*.'

'Who?'

Crofts hesitated then, still unsure. 'I was thinking of Simpson.'

It was her turn to stare. 'But he was responsible for your coming here in the first place, Mike. Perhaps . . . perhaps he even killed Eric himself. How can you trust him of all people?'

'It's a question of priorities. If Simpson was involved in Eric's death, then we'll sort out the bastard later. But right now we need a friend at court – an unquestionably loyal friend. Simpson *has* to be cleared to Top Secret by MOD Security: they've never have allowed him near Ardarroch if he'd shown any leanings towards Soviet contacts. And he's ex-Royal Navy: already tuned to the "old boy" net. He has the contacts and carries the rank to keep things low key. He's also a gambler, Laura. And we need a gambler.'

Oh, all right; so there was a warning bell still tinkling faintly at the back of his mind. He'd known Eric a lot more intimately than Simpson, and look what had happened to loyalties there . . . but he had to take this one chance. Just this one. He didn't know a lot about its capabilities as a weapon, but even the little he'd guessed about Spearfish was beginning to frighten him too much.

Laura said, 'But I thought you couldn't get through to Simpson at Ardarroch, Mike. You can hardly walk through the gates and demand to see him.'

He smiled grimly.

'I might just have a way,' he said, reaching for the telephone again, 'for one non-existent man to make contact with another.'

'Navy Ardarroch. Can I help you, sir?'

It was a female voice this time: probably a WRNS operator. Crofts kept his voice casual. 'Commander Edward Simpson, please.'

There was only the slightest hesitation. She must have been an efficient operator: apparently she knew the name of every staff member, even daily visitors, without having to think. Or had she been briefed on what to deny?

'We have no Commander Simpson aboard, sir. Can anyone else be of assistance?'

Crofts said, 'I think you should confirm you haven't with your duty officer, miss. Before I hang up on you . . . And when you've checked that Commander Simpson isn't there, perhaps you'd tell him a Mister Thomson is calling. From Copenhagen.'

'One minute please, sir.'

It didn't take a whole minute. Simpson's voice came on the line within thirty seconds. Brittle and very wary.

'Who's calling. Or is this a joke?'

'No,' Crofts assured him truthfully. 'It isn't a joke, Simpson.'

'Crofts?'

'Your memory's much better,' Crofts said with heavy irony. 'The last time we spoke you had difficulty in recognising me, never mind my voice.'

'Thomson – calling from Copenhagen.' Simpson was cool now; beginning to spar. 'Whatever caused you to use that name, Crofts?'

'I'm talking to you, aren't I?' Crofts retorted.

There was a momentary silence. Then, 'I've been hearing rather disturbing things about you, old boy. You've made quite a mark for yourself up here: all the morning papers are full of you.'

'You shouldn't believe everything you read in the papers,' Crofts chided him. 'Any more than I should have believed an accidental meeting with an old acquaintance *was* accidental.'

'Look,' Simpson interjected smoothly, changing the subject. 'I don't know where you are – and I've no intention of having this call traced, by the way, old son – but if I were in your unenviable shoes, then I rather think I *would* be telephoning from Copenhagen. Or even further away from these sceptred isles. Speculation has it that the local constabulary are somewhat annoyed with you, particularly since you apparently insist on scattering dead bobbies around the Highlands.'

'So you want me to go away as well, do you, Commander? I did wonder what your feelings would be in that respect.'

'Ambiguous. No intense concern for you, old boy; merely a word of friendly advice from a campaign comrade. And if it helps, then I'm genuinely sorry about Major Harley: I'm sure you didn't mean to kill him . . .'

'Crap!' Crofts broke in tightly. 'Like everything else you've said so far, Simpson. Maybe you should just try asking why I've telephoned instead of lying through your teeth.'

'I'm sure I don't know what you mean,' Simpson echoed with an almost believable note of injury. 'But go ahead – do tell me?'

Crofts drew a deep breath. He was about to play his only ace. 'Spearfish,' he said tensely. 'I'm calling you about Spearfish, Commander.'

He waited for the explosion, but it never came. In fact when Simpson spoke again it was with a certain amusement. 'An odd preoccupation for a chap in your position. Still – what would you like to know about it, Crofts? It's a Top Secret lightweight torpedo currently being evaluated for acceptance by the Royal Navy. Absolutely years ahead of its time. Give you bags of detail if you're really keen – length, weight, technical bits about the revolutionary new battery Chloride's developed to power the whizzer; streets ahead of the jobs we power the present Mark 33's with . . .'

'Simpson,' Crofts muttered weakly. 'Simpson – why the hell are you telling me about . . .'

'. . . thing virtually thinks for itself, y'know. We've stuck in a microprocessor controlled multi-mode, multi-beam sonar functioning through thirty-one elements in the creature's nose. Gallops off programmed with a shopping list of Soviet targets and just hunts around till it scores. Absolute torpedo man's dream.'

Crofts stared blankly at Laura. Her eyes were fixed on his and she could see something was wrong. She said, 'What, Mike? What's he saying, for God's sake?'

'He's describing it to me. On the telephone,' Crofts whispered disbelievingly.

'Of course we've been programming it for years. Every Ivan nuke passing through the Greenland-Iceland gap's been signatured and sound-characterised. Our little fish'll carry a friend or foe profile plus an ability to employ alternating sonar frequencies against Red Force counter-measures vessels. . . '

'Simpson!' Crofts roared. 'You just said it yourself – it's bloody Top *Secret*, man!'

The voice on the other end of the line ground to a halt.

'Of course it is,' Simpson protested, rather put out.

Crofts blinked. 'Well?'

'Well what?'

'But you're *talking* about it, Simpson. Telling me all about Spearfish!'

Simpson chuckled. 'Where have you been for the last few years, Crofts.'

Crofts said, 'Africa.'

'Ah, that explains it. Lord, this is Britain, old boy: we don't have any secrets from the great British public . . . or only tiny ones, anyway. *The Times* and the *Guardian* and those other great protectors of the treasury purse have been speculating on Spearfish for months now. "Will dear old Auntie MOD buy British; or will we go for some updated US Navy job because of the political pressures?" Oh no, Crofts: don't think that Spearfish's existence is secret – it's not. Come to that, any Soviet spy can order himself a copy of *Western Defence Revue* and read all about it for a modest outlay. It's the way we work in the free world, old boy. Saves the KGB an enormous amount of effort.'

Crofts knew then that Simpson was playing a deeper game. The real secrets of Spearfish – the true technology behind the weapon – were still concealed by the high wire fences of Ardarroch. They didn't give them away for the price of a magazine: not the real Machiavellian gut of the thing.

'Simpson,' he said, slowly and deliberately. 'Your Spearfish is about to be hijacked. Probably within the next forty-eight hours.'

This time there was a much longer silence. When Simpson

did reply there was no hint of amusement any more. On the other hand he didn't quite react in the way Crofts had expected, either.

'That allegation I do have to take seriously, Crofts. At the same time I have to remind you of the existence of the Official Secrets Act. For one thing this is an open GPO line – hardly a secure means of discussing highly classified material.'

'With four murder charges hanging over my head,' Crofts growled, 'I'm hardly overawed by any penalties threatened by the Official Secrets Act. Besides, I thought you claimed you didn't have any secrets in this brave free western world of yours.'

'Don't be *bloody* facetious!' Simpson retorted. 'Now look, old boy, *I'm* bound by the wretched rules, like it or not. I really can't discuss security affairs on the phone: we've got to meet – obviously somewhere quiet. Safe from your point of view.'

Something made Crofts hesitate. It all seemed too easy. Simpson hadn't asked the questions any reasonable man would have put before committing himself to a tryst with an alleged mass-murderer. He hadn't pressed Crofts on the killings: he hadn't expressed quite enough surprise at the use of the scientist, Thomson's, name. Was this because Simpson knew enough about Crofts to trust him – or because Simpson already knew the answers?

Quickly he covered the receiver and caught Laura's eye. 'Do you have the Land Rover here?'

She frowned. 'Yes.'

'Oban: I don't know Oban. Suggest a public place.'

'The . . . post office. On Albany Street. Why?'

But he was talking to the phone again. 'Meet me in Oban.'

He hoped Simpson really hadn't been tracing the call: his decision had been a spontaneous one. The warning bell was ringing at the back of his mind again. More and more Crofts was beginning to suspect that the Strathclyde police might pose less of a threat to his safety than would a meeting with Simpson at some isolated rendezvous in the mountains.

'Oban?' Simpson's voice betrayed a certain surprise. Or

was it disconcertion? 'Look, old boy, is that really wise?'

'One hour,' Crofts snapped. 'In front of the Albany Street post office. And come alone, Simpson: no public-spirited backup.'

Simpson's protest was mildly indignant. '*I'm* not MOD Plod or any other variety of policeman, old boy. I'm totally indifferent as to how you settle your personal affairs . . .'

Crofts slammed the phone down and met Laura's anxious eye.

'How do you propose to get across the pavement and into the Rover in daylight, Mike? With the police station virtually next door?'

He shrugged his shoulders with a reassuring lightness he didn't feel. 'The same way as I intend to loiter on a street corner in full view of the Oban constabulary – brazenly, an' nervous as hell.'

He was correct in thinking it had all seemed too easy; far too uncomplicated by the standards of the Spearfish affair.

They'd driven into Oban like a pair of day-trip tourists: it might even have been a pleasant outing had Crofts not suddenly realised they were following precisely the same road as that of last night. When Woollen Men had destroyed Chequered-cap men before vanishing as though they'd never been.

The white police vehicle had gone when they passed the killing ground, but dark uniformed figures in gumboots still combed the surrounding gorse. Crofts should have been challenged then; recognised and stopped as the price of his recklessness. Only he wasn't. Instead, the solitary constable on duty by the road waved them impatiently past while Laura shrank behind the wheel and Crofts gripped the Beretta below the dashboard with a grim prayer that he wouldn't be called upon to use it.

For he would have done, had the need arisen. Perhaps not to kill: not another young policeman . . . but certainly to make his last desperate stand a memorable one in the annals of the Strathclyde Constabulary. Crofts was a determined man now; and becoming more and more determined as his resentment against those who had crucified him grew ever more intense.

Finally they were driving into Oban itself, entering by the road from Connel Bridge and negotiating the early-season George Street tourists. Crofts sensed his chances of avoiding detection were increasing by the minute: no police officer would be likely to pick him from that transient, idling crowd.

They parked the Rover near Argyll Square and walked to the General Post Office. It was nearly two o'clock when the sun came out, and its spring warmth played on their faces as they waited anxiously for the arrival of Simpson.

They needed Commander Simpson RN so desperately. Simpson held the key. Oh, Simpson could easily secure Crofts' arrest were he so minded, but currently Crofts must surely hold the upper hand. Spearfish itself was at risk, and only he knew the method of its compromise: about the darkened craft and Quarry Cove, and the airfield of Tarvit Farm.

Simpson must, therefore, be prepared at least to listen to them: to offer co-operation in return for information. And Simpson of all people was the best placed to do that.

Come on, Simpson. C'mon Simpson . . .

'Crofts: Mrs Harley? I trust you haven't been kept waiting too long.'

They turned quickly; eyeing the tall, elegant figure which had apparently materialised from nowhere. Crofts felt the reassuring coldness of the Beretta's grip inside his raincoat pocket. He didn't return the quizzical smile.

'Hello, Simpson,' he said, looking past Simpson's shoulder and suspiciously scanning the faces of the passers-by. He hoped he wasn't going to have to shoot Simpson. Not here; in the middle of Oban.

Mind you, he had the uneasy feeling he was going to have to shoot *somebody* for killing Eric. And probably very soon.

CHAPTER SEVENTEEN

He hadn't changed since their meeting in Selfridges – Commander Simpson. He still looked very ordinary, and not at all like the buccaneer of the Mekong Delta. The pinstripe, the black jacket, bowler hat; the City unbrella of course, neatly furled and hooked over one languid arm . . . Crofts suddenly noticed Simpson's eyes: how extraordinarily colourless they were.

He was carrying a cheap plastic supermarket carrier bag in his other hand. It looked a bit out of place against the rest of Simpson, and it also reminded Crofts of his own earlier expedition in London – when he'd tried so unimaginatively to conceal Beretta M951 while searching for what he'd then assumed would prove its final burial ground.

Simpson turned politely to Laura. 'I really mustn't keep you long,' he said. 'So do please forgive me, Mrs Harley, if I address myself solely to our mutual friend . . .'

'Spearfish, Simpson,' Crofts rasped. 'Where do you fit into the official scheme of things?'

Simpson's pale eyes didn't even flicker. 'Don't ask, Crofts. Let's say I'm simply here to tender advice: not information.'

'Oh, no!' Crofts shook his head. Part of the reason he was in this mess was because he'd already accepted Simpson's 'advice' without question, so subtly delivered in London. 'Not this time, Commander.'

'Advice?' Laura interjected quickly, forstalling the imminent explosion. And of course she was right: they only stood to gain from encouraging Simpson to talk freely; certainly more than they would if Crofts began waving guns in full view of the Oban tourist trade – apart from the immediate police presence such an extraordinary display would invite.

'Well-intentioned advice, Mrs Harley.' Simpson jiggled the plastic shopping bag sardonically. 'Accompanied by a small token of esteem on behalf of those bearing our mutual friend's best interests at heart.'

An elderly lady hesitated as she left the post office, uncertain of whether or not to pass between them. Commander Edward Simpson RN stepped aside, politely raising his bowler hat. The lady smiled appreciatively – it was a sad reflection on the world that there were all too few gentlemen like Commander Simpson left – and entering the passing crowd while her *gallant* rejoined the conversation.

'This token of sincerity,' Crofts growled, eyeing the plastic bag with the wary contempt of the forewarned. 'What calibre of token is it, Simpson?'

Simpson grinned. He didn't even pretend to look hurt. 'This *is* Oban, old boy; not Vietnam.'

'Look in the bag, Laura,' Crofts snapped, lining his concealed Beretta on the third button from the top of Simpson's waistcoat. 'Carefully.'

'It's money,' Laura said blankly a few moments later. 'American money, I think.'

'Ten thousand US dollars,' their urbane associate added, helpfully. 'A thoroughly flexible international currency.'

Crofts fixed him with a baleful eye. He didn't really need to ask; the message already bore a weary familiarity. But he asked anyway.

'Meaning?'

'Use it to travel, old boy. It could transport you some considerable distance from the nearest British bobby; even utilising the more expensive, if somewhat . . . ah . . . clandestine, channels still open to you.'

'Did you supply the money? Along with the advice?'

'Official Secrets Act, old son – remember? Any further amplification would cause me to exceed my terms of reference. Just look on me as a solicitous bearer of good will.'

Crofts blinked disbelievingly as Simpson tipped his bowler hat to the equally-discomfited Laura and, well . . . quite simply, turned to go. Hurriedly he stepped forward.

'Glance down towards my raincoat pocket before you walk away. Simpson. And don't persuade yourself I won't use it to spoil the rest of your afternoon.'

Simpson did, and then looked bleak. He didn't appear to have any doubts. 'Aren't we being a bit melodramatic, Crofts?'

'I don't know. It all depends on whether you think blowing the base of someone's spine away in public *does* constitute melodrama. Old boy.'

'Stay out of it, Crofts. Take the money and run.'

'You should have said that earlier. When we first met . . . Now, let's talk about Spearfish, Commander. What's your official interest in it? More particularly, why did you deliberately steer me towards Eric Harley and Auchenzie, while now you only want me to disappear? Why, come to that, does Scarred-Hand seem equally more intent on encouraging my departure, rather than my capture . . .'

'Scarred-who?' Simpson asked blankly.

'I don't *know* "who",' Crofts snarled almost plaintively. 'That's why we're bloody here, Simpson. To find out!'

A whole family carrying ice creams and wearing plastic macs pushed between them. Crofts gripped the Beretta convulsively, suddenly masked from his target, but Simpson didn't move. When the determined holiday-makers had passed through he was still there; grinning almost sympathetically at Crofts' discomfiture. The piratical touch was firmly re-established.

'Maybe we should stroll somewhere a little less busy, old boy?' Commander Simpson suggested helpfully. 'People getting in the way: it could prove difficult – shooting me in this crowd.'

The blue-mist Western Highland afternoon was already drawing to a close when the three of them stood before the wedding-cake hotels lining Corran Esplanade. To their left projected Railway Pier with its cluster of shipping; to the north, spectral in the haze, stood the black ruins of Dunollie

Castle, bleak and forbidding on their bold promontory, a tragic bequest from the great Lords of Lorne who had owned near one third of Scotland in their day. Westwards the first fingers of evening were reaching fast across the Firth; the Sound of Mull dark and emphasising the anxious sparks of navigation buoys flickering their mariner's caution.

There were very few strollers here to face the chill breeze of early season Oban. Simpson held his hands wide in sardonic anticipation, furled umbrella dangling casually from his arm. 'No concealed weapons, Crofts. You'll have to take my word for it that we're not under surveillance.'

Laura pressed on, 'You've already trusted the Commander this far, Michael. They could have arrested you a long time ago if he'd intended them to.'

Crofts eyed Simpson expressionlessly, then withdrew his hand from his pocket. 'All right. But I'm not going to run, Simpson: I'm staying around until I find answers. Accept that, and we'll both save a lot of sparring.'

It was the tall naval officer's turn to stare calculatingly. Then he shrugged. 'Affirmative . . . If I consider your questions pertinent.'

'Are you working for the British security services? Is that why you're involved at Ardarroch trials range?'

'For Naval counter-intelligence. Yes.'

'Spearfish – you already know it's the target for a heist?'

'We know the Soviets have sanctioned an operation to compromise it. We know they have a team established in the area . . .'

'At Den of Tarvit? Harley's place?'

'Yes.'

Simpson turned as Laura gave a little cry. He wasn't being flippant any longer. 'Hear us out, Mrs Harley. Please.'

'Then your own people – the British – must have killed Eric,' Crofts concluded bitterly. 'If he was working for the Russians.'

'I didn't say that, Crofts,' Simpson retorted spiritedly. 'Eric Harley was working for us – undercover. Your husband was a patriot, Mrs Harley. I'm sorry he's dead, but he did die with honour. It's a knowledge which may comfort you a little.'

Sudden tears glinted in Laura's eyes but she still managed a whisper. 'Thank you, Commander.'

So Eric Harley *hadn't* been a traitor after all. Crofts felt a futile gladness for Laura – for himself, for that matter – but there were still too many questions; too many pieces of the Auchenzie jigsaw still loose on the board.

'His murder, then,' he pressed. 'Someone in the Soviet team?'

Simpson shrugged and looked grim. 'Presumably. They're making the hit soon. Your friend might even have been trying to get word to me when he was surprised.'

'Tomorrow night,' Crofts muttered absently. 'We think that's when they plan to do it.'

The colourless eyes transfixed him. There was something there, deep down inside them, but Crofts couldn't analyse it. 'I think you'd better tell me what else you know,' Simpson probed grimly.

'It's probably to take place at sea, then the torpedo will be flown out from the Tarvit airstrip . . .'

Crofts hesitated. The element in Simpson's gaze was one of concern. But was that simply for the security of Spearfish – or because of the extent of Crofts' knowledge? His wariness returned and, along with it, his anger.

'My questions first, Simpson. Then I'll give you what you need . . . How does Harry Mearns fit in?'

'Ostensibly as a retired colonial, come home to roost, like yourself and Eric Harley. In reality, still working – but for Soviet paymasters. Same with his three teamsters. The Politburo didn't dare risk using assault-trained KGB on the UK mainland . . . Luckily for us they were careless enough to pick on someone like Harley, who had enough conscience to blow the whistle on the plan.'

'Which of them d'you think killed him?' Crofts snapped.

'If you want a guess – Harry Mearns.'

'Mearns couldn't have done it,' Laura said quietly. 'Nor any of his trio. They were all with us at the time.'

'And Scarred-Hand unwittingly convinced me that *his*

crowd weren't involved,' Crofts interjected. 'But then, you claim not to know who they are, don't you, Simpson?'

The Commander shrugged the inference aside. 'I hesitate to state the obvious, Mrs Harley,' he remarked smoothly, 'but I have no proof that Crofts here is quite as innocent as his self-righteous indignation proclaims. Nor, for that matter, have the police; or presumably they wouldn't have arrested him.'

'I did not . . . kill . . . Eric!' Crofts grated dangerously.

'Of course not, old boy. Any more than you blew away those two policemen. Or the Boer, Mulders . . .'

'How do *you* know about Mulders' death?' Crofts challenged quickly. 'That was only discovered this morning. Too late for the press to publicise.'

Simpson's eyes flickered again then, but he recovered with a smile. 'Car radio, old boy. Currently you're topic for the day on Radio Clyde.'

Crofts gazed at his adversary. Curious: why did he think of Simpson in terms of being an 'adversary'? Everything seemed to fit so far. The wind came down from the Firth of Lorne and snatched with chilled fingers at his hair, but he didn't feel it. There was still something unexplained; something which niggled in the back of his mind about Simpson.

'Why are you so anxious – ten thousand dollars anxious – to keep me on the run?' he asked. 'Why, for that matter, did you entice me up here in the first place, Simpson? It *was* deliberately contrived, wasn't it? Our meeting in Selfridges.'

'The money belongs to the great British taxpayer, old son.' Simpson grinned deprecatingly, 'Much as I'd like to claim it was to help an old comrade, it wouldn't be true. And MOD want to encourage you to stay on the run because they don't want Police Constable Plod poking into national security affairs, trying to substantiate the story you'd be bound to tell 'em if you're caught. We daren't risk the KGB being frightened off at this stage of the game – we want them in the bag as soon as they put their sticky Marxist hands out for Spearfish. We'd like some proof with which we can embarrass the Kremlin to such an extent they'll shy away from torpedo-stealing for a very long time.'

. . . which made sense. Indeed, it presented a similar line of argument to that of Laura's earlier. While the police were hunting Crofts, they wouldn't be searching for any deeper significance behind Eric Harley's murder.

'You didn't answer the second part of my question – about your enticing me up here? An innocent blundering into what seems to be a hive of espionage.'

'My own initiative: I hoped your gut-suspicions would offer Eric Harley some protection. Look, I'm a naval officer, Crofts; I have to stick to the rules. The Secrets Act didn't permit me to tell you the reasons why.'

'. . . mine but to do – and die!' Crofts muttered savagely. 'Christ, man; I didn't even carry a gun!'

'Harley *was* killed with your Beretta, old boy. We only have your word you didn't bring it with you.'

Crofts still glowered, full of resentment. 'Well, you could've briefed me a *little* mo . . . !'

And *then* it hit him. Beretta M951! He'd always considered it a possibility that Simpson was connected with Eric's murder, but only now did he realise he had proof. Simpson had been aware of his presence in London before it all began – out of all the mystery groups, only Simpson was *known* to have been in a position to have retrieved the Beretta's dismembered parts. And the next occasion on which he'd come across that same weapon was in the farmhouse at Den of Tarvit. Lying next to Eric Harley's shattered corpse . . . !'

But at this early stage nobody, other than the police officers investigating the violence at Tarvit Farm, could possibly have been aware of the *make* of weapon used by the killer. Certainly THAT information hadn't been broadcast on Radio Clyde!

Simpson must have read the expression on Crofts' face because he stepped back a wary pace, steadying the furled umbrella still crooked over his arm. Laura let out a startled cry as Crofts grabbed for Simpson, ignoring, in his blind fury, the gun in his pocket; wanting only to lunge at Simpson, strike blindly at the man now surely exposed as having been responsible for the murder of Eric Harley.

'It WAS you, you bastard! It had to be *British* Security who blew Eric away!'

But Simpson was also moving; twisting from Crofts' reach with an agility which belied his city softness. Briefly, in that moment of startled self-reproach at his own foolishness, Crofts glimpsed the eyes. They weren't the eyes of a gentlemanly naval officer any more: now they were hooded, ugly; the colourless eyes of a striking snake.

Laura screamed, 'Mike! The *umbrella!*'

. . . and then Crofts saw it: the minute glitter of some alien device located within the point of the umbrella as Simpson's hand came round, gripping the brolly expertly by its leather-encased handle, levelling the black-furled accessory with the delicate balance of a rapier blade . . . lunging for Crofts' face!

Crofts panicked, blurted '*Jesus!*' and hurled himself sideways, at the same time grabbing in reflex desperation for the makeshift weapon. Miraculously his hand clamped around its slender folds; snatching it more by sheer luck than intent from Simpson's grasp.

But then he was gone – Commander Edward Simpson, Royal Navy. Scattering the few knots of strollers prepared to brave the Atlantic breezes, black coat flapping, dapper-striped trouser legs reciprocating pistons . . . Crofts gaped after him for a moment, knowing he daren't shoot for fear of hitting those gaping pedestrians, yet not certain what to do next. It had been such a bizarre encounter; a still fairly unbelievable incident in a totally unbelievable saga.

But they, too, couldn't delay. Ashen-faced, Laura whispered an urgent, 'Two policemen, Mike! Coming from the castle direction. They're bound to be curious.'

Crofts examined the tip of Simpson's sartorial legacy as they walked hurriedly towards the bustle of Railway Pier. His mortification was absolute: he'd committed the most elementary error in the military manual; the sort one would anticipate only from some thistledown-chinned subaltern. Not only had he overlooked the strength, the expertise and above all, the determination of his enemy, but he'd also blundered naively into an engagement with a man who'd come fully-equipped for professional assassination.

It appeared that there was nothing makeshift at all about the umbrella of Simpson RN.

There was a short, seemingly hollow needle projecting from its tip; apparently laughable as a threat to anything more formidable than a butterfly. But Crofts carried it very, very carefully from then on. It seemed a fair assumption that the needle had been treated in some diabolical manner; with, say, some lethal derivative from the cauldrons of chemical warfare.

For Crofts remembered, too late, a certain Vietnamese sampan of many years before. And the way that a buc-caneering naval officer had managed to turn even *that* innocuous peasant craft into a most efficient killing machine.

They hunted for some time, but Crofts already knew they would never find Simpson again. Also, by staying in Oban, he fully realised the foolish risk he was running; revealing himself in an area where every approaching step might be the step of a policeman. But they had few alternatives left now. Simpson had promised to be their only real hope, yet Simpson had proved even more of an enigma than before.

So the situation had become even more confusing. If Simpson *was* a British counter-intelligence man – and surely that had to be the truth, for why else would Simpson have had access to MOD Ardarroch? – then why had Simpson run when Crofts had confronted him? Why not call in the Marines: overwhelm Crofts; use the power of authority so obviously his?

Or did that again raise doubts about what, precisely, *was* Simpson's interest in the thinking torpedo of Ardarroch? Certainly it couldn't be identical to that of Harry Mearns. And there was still the complication of Scarred-Hand and his Woollen Men. Where the hell did those monsters fit in? Were *they* working with Simpson despite his denial. Or with Mearns. Or against them both?

Crofts turned uncertainly, staring out over the yachts moored in the bay. There were few out there yet; the winter gales were only fading now. A bigger hull closed slowly on the Railway Pier, windows yellow as moonlit tigers' teeth along her high superstructure: the Oban car ferry returning from its regular service to the Inner Islands and Mull. Fishing boats still jostled for overnight berths, while further down the quayside a Norwegian oil rig tender lay in a generator-throbbing pool of after deck-lights. The oilmen were gradually consolidating on the west coast; already they built many of their monstrous structures where once only salmon had swum and ospreys plunged; soon they would be clamping the first wellheads to the bed of the cold grey sea itself.

'Mike.'

Laura's hand stole into Crofts', but it was an anxious squeeze without any more romantic implication. 'Mike, you shouldn't be taking so many risks.'

'D'you see that boat lying down there,' he interrupted suddenly. 'Down past the oil supply job?'

She squinted; shading her eyes against the glare. 'The lights are too bright to . . .'

But Crofts had gone, striding urgently ahead. When she finally caught up with him, he was already sheltering discreetly beside a stack of orange plastic fish boxes; secure in the shadows cast by the Norwegian's cargo lamps and staring down at the last vessel in line.

She was wooden built; a powerful-looking hard-chine craft maybe thirty to thirty-three metres overall with a vaguely ex-military air about her. Scandinavian perhaps; the sort of thing the Swedes might once have deployed in island patrolling, with the wide clear deck spaces where Oerlikon and depth charge rack could well have found a mount. Now she was unarmed and inoffensive: a typical survey ship conversion run on a shoestring like many cruising on the fringes of wherever oilmen gather; littered with diving gear and marker buoys and a Gemini-type inflatable tender, a single two-ton derrick and a black-greased disarray of wires to foul her once streamed lines. A dirty ship under the pressures of commerce with a faded courtesy Ensign dangling limp from her single mast and no flag at her counter.

She did bear a name though, and even a port of registry of sorts – displayed in peeling letters on a lifebuoy against her bridge. *Marauder: Panama*.

Crofts had heard that name once before, and very recently. Earlier that same morning in fact, while an only-too-brief acquaintance was spending his last conscious moments amidst this mortal coil. *Marauder* – according to the reluctant confession of the late unlamented Boer Mulders – was the name of the dark silhouette Crofts had observed entering Quarry Cove.

And there was more. Even as Crofts and Laura pressed back against the shadows and Crofts touched, with abruptly revitalised hope, upon the cold comfort of Beretta M951 concealed within his coat, a door opened from forward of the bridge and two men stepped across the coaming to the deck.

Despite the fading light the first was already more than familiar, both to Crofts and to Laura – it was the second who caused them both to frown without recognition. Until the pair moved forward into the fizzling glare from the service vessel's arc lamps, briefly clasping hands as the first man prepared to depart . . . whereupon Laura uttered a funny, curiously frightened gasp and blurted, 'Look, Mike – the other man's *wrist*!'

And they discovered they had fitted two further pieces of the jigsaw together: neatly interlocked on this occasion. Oh, of course Harry Mearns was one – hardly a surprise: his connection with the night ship had already been established. But the other – in all probability the captain of *Marauder* himself – had simultaneously provided them with a face where before had existed only a target for their anger and frustration.

Crofts felt good. He would know now where to find that second man whenever it came time to kill him.

The callous alien. The one whom, until that pleasurable moment, he'd been forced to label simply as Scarred-Hand.

The previously hooded director-general of the Woollen Men!

It was vitally important to keep track of Mearns, who now presented their only vulnerable source of information.

They hurried to collect the Land Rover, then Laura drove back to the Railway Pier. They didn't have to wait long: Harry soon appeared, wandering idly from *Marauder*'s berth with casual interest. Laura pulled forward until he was abreast, then braked suddenly and peeped the horn.

'Hello, Mister Mearns. Whatever are you doing here in Oban?'

Mearns halted, peering not without a certain caution through the open window. It was only when he saw Laura alone that he relaxed perceptibly.

'Mrs Harley. I . . . ah, thought I'd get away for an hour or two. After last night and, well, what happened.'

'I felt the same,' Laura said, and there was no falsehood in the glinting eyes. 'I couldn't stay at the farm alone.'

Harry shuffled awkwardly, probably in genuine embarrassment. He'd seen a plethora of war widows – had, for that matter, created quite a few himself – but he wasn't too used to dealing with proper ladies.

'I'm sorry. About your husband, Mrs Harley. He was a good bloke.'

There were a few weary travellers drifting towards them along the pier, disembarking from the Island steamer. Laura frowned with pretended concern. 'How are you getting back to Auchenzie, Harry. Where's your car?'

'Over by the North Pier. I'm on my way to pick it up. Thought I'd take a gander at the boats first. Just passing time.'

'Get in, I'll run you across.'

Harry came round the bonnet and opened the passenger's door, then hesitated. Maybe the meeting was ringing alarm bells with Harry too, by then; just too neat a coincidence for the battle-wise mind of Company Sergeant Major Mearns.

'Thanks, Mrs Harley, but on second thoughts – no. Maybe I'll jus' wander a bit mo . . .'

Crofts didn't actually have to use words. There were much quicker ways of emphasising reality to Harry Mearns. He simply lifted the canvas drop they'd unstrapped between front and rear compartments and jerked the muzzle of the Beretta invitingly. Harry got in and sat staring straight ahead while a suddenly tight-lipped Laura engaged the clutch.

It was only after they'd passed Connel Bridge and were driving along the now dark road to Auchenzie that Harry finally spoke. Quite placidly. Just as Crofts would have expected him to.

'You goin' to shoot me then, Major?' Harry asked.

Crofts didn't even smile at the back of his ex-CSM's head. 'Probably.'

Mearns turned then and gave him a quizzical stare; a defiant, almost challenging grin which ignored the Beretta's rock-steady eye. Crofts knew exactly what was in his mind: he was thinking of Angola just over a year ago; of Crofts' hesitancy to pull the trigger on Hermann Bosche, and wondering if it was worth a gamble.

Crofts hoped Harry wouldn't decide it was. Too much had happened since then; too many of the few illusions he'd still had left had finally been betrayed. Laura too had already suffered enough horror. He didn't think she could survive the added trauma of having a human brain exploding right beside her. But the man had guts; Crofts had to allow him that. Or was victim of an even more dangerous madness: he'd never really been a hundred per cent sure; not in all the years he'd fought on the same side as Harry.

At least in the years in which he'd *thought* he'd been fighting on the same side as Harry.

Or had that been *another* bloody illusion? He'd never quite been sure about that, either.

Tarvit Farm was dark and deserted when they circumspectly approached. As expected, the police had gone, and so had all traces of their calling. Crofts was glad of that, too. He wanted light for his chat with Harry, he wanted to be able to look into Harry Mearns' eyes, and Tarvit was the only place he knew where there was light without life. Light, and now the sadness of misplaced hope.

Laura stayed outside with the Rover. She'd claimed she preferred to; to be able to warn them if any other vehicle approached. Or maybe she just couldn't face that tiny, neatly furnished room where Eric had been shot to death. Crofts could face it, though. Crofts needed all his anger.

He sat Harry down in Eric's chair, and stared at him across the gun, waiting. Mearns knew it was his cue. He wasn't nervous even then: merely practical.

'Money, Major? We all work for money, huh?'

Crofts shook his head. He already had ten thousand dollars thrown carelessly into the back of the Rover: Simpson's money. It didn't dilute his hate one bit.

'It's about Spearfish!' he said. 'Tell me all about Spearfish and Quarry Cove first, Harry.'

Harry's eyes showed surprise, displaced by wry amusement. 'I told Harley to get rid of you that first day. He should've done. You always were an inquisitive bastard, Crofts: particularly in the middle of the night.'

'Spearfish, Mearns. Without the frills.'

'O.K. So we're going to heist it. But I guess you've figured that much for yourself. What else is there to tell?'

'Everything. How, why, when . . . and who for. Particularly who for. You're working for the Soviets, aren't you?'

Mearns looked startled. 'What put that idea into your head?'

'Just answer the question, Mearns. Have you been hired by the KGB?'

'Christ, you've been reading too many novels since you retired.'

Crofts sighed. 'I think I'm going to have to shoot you very soon, Harry.'

Mearns' eyes hardened a fraction; mocking Crofts. 'It was you who didn't have the guts to pull the trigger on Hermann the German, remember?'

Crofts lifted the Beretta muzzle. 'Don't bet on it too heavily, Harry. Answer the question – are you working for the Soviets?'

'Negative.'

'Then who?'

Mearns grinned; very much the old, unabashed Harry.

'Ourselves.'

Even Crofts had to smile at that: without a lot of humour, though. Then he leaned forward and levelled the gun on Harry's forehead. 'Cheerio, Harry.'

'Listen, dammit!' Mearns snapped urgently. 'Think about what Spearfish means, Major.'

'What does it mean, Harry? Help me a little.'

Mearns eyed the gun pointedly and Crofts slowly lowered it again. He didn't want Harry to be too nervous. Harry told a much better story when he was happy.

'First,' Harry Mearns growled, 'you got to understand its market value. It makes Exocet, Sidewinder, Sea Wolf look like stones from a kid's catapult by comparison. That Spearfish tool is death to any Soviet submarine – hell, d'you know what its SSKC is, Crofts; its single shot kill capability? I'll tell you, friend – ninety-eight per cent! The contractors an' the Royal Navy have been programming it for four years: they've built every conceivable avoiding action a Russian nuke captain could ever devise into its brain. It out-thinks, outmanoeuvres him every bloody time once it's launched – and it travels faster through the water than any submerged sub ever will.'

'O.K., so it's a high-efficiency weapon. All you've done is underline the Soviet's need to go for it. To the Kremlin it's worth every rouble they have to pay to a mercenary hit squad to grab it for them . . .'

'Or worth every pound sterling the British Government would be prepared to pay,' Harry interposed, 'for those same mercenaries *not* to hand it over to Ivan.'

Crofts' eyes narrowed. He was beginning to understand what Mearns was driving at. 'You're claiming the Russians aren't involved: that this hijack is solely a criminal proposition? Kidnapping – but a torpedo instead of some millionaire's kid?'

Harry gave a mocking bow from his chair. 'Clever, eh? We're figuring to heist Spearfish as a strictly commercial blackmail operation. Hijack, hide – and demand a ransom for its return from an embarrassed British Goverment. And you can bet they'll pay damn quick, Major – before any NATO allies have time to discover how careless they've been with Top Secret secrets.'

'You said "hijack and hide",' Crofts interjected sharply. 'Hide where, Harry?'

'In the Irish Republic.'

'Flown out from the Tarvit airstrip the same night?'

'You have been an inquisitive bastard,' Mearns commented cheerfully.

Crofts stared long and hard at Harry Mearns then. It did make sense; good sense. There were still gaps, though.

'What about Scarred-Hand? Where do his team fit in?'

'Scarred-who?'

'The *Marauder* crowd. You're working with them, Harry, yet they're out of your league. You and me, we never were too keen on boats. Who fitted you out with a navy?'

Mearns shook his head. 'I don't know who's paymaster: who's right at the top. The instructions were passed through Eric Harley – I'm just the dumb bloody sergeant major, remember? I'm not supposed to be able to think, Crofts: it's the "officers" like you an' Harley who do that.'

And the vitriol in Harry's tone persuaded Crofts that this, at least, was the truth.

'And the *Marauder* team?'

'Mercenaries too. Never came across any of them in the Africa trade. Mostly Finns and Scowegians except, perhaps, for Andersen, your scarred-hand merchant. He's their captain, and a right evil bastard.'

'You'll get on well with him then, Harry,' Crofts said expressionlessly. 'They killed the two policemen; did you know that?'

Harry shrugged. 'Not before they'd done it.'

'Why did they do it, Harry; then deliberately set me up? Was it to keep the police chasing after me for a straight drunken murder so's they didn't dig any deeper and come up with a major criminal operation . . .'

. . . And that was when it hit Crofts. When it all began to

tie in. He felt his hand shaking as the hate stirred within him again.

Mearns didn't notice right away. 'They don't have to give reasons to me. I'm just the hired help . . .'

His voice trailed off. Crofts had risen to his feet and was crossing the room towards him. For the first time Harry Mearns' eyes showed a flicker of fear. Especially when Crofts placed the muzzle of the Beretta hard under his right ear, forcing his head to one side.

But Crofts had suddenly developed A Suspicion. A Suspicion which made him very angry indeed.

Say he'd been wrong about Simpson's involvement. Say Andersen *had* shot Eric after all, had spotted him as a British undercover man.

'Harry,' Crofts said slowly. 'Tell me, Harry, was it you who put the finger on Eric. And then stood and drank beer while Scarred-Hand blew him away?'

Mearns shook his head carefully. He'd learned many years before that Beretta M951 had an unsettlingly light trigger pressure. 'Aw, f'r Christ's sake, Crofts – no, I didn't!'

'You're dead, Harry,' Crofts promised. 'I'm going to count to five – and then you're dead. Just like Hermann Bosche.'

'Leave it, Crofts! Leave the bloody speculation alone.'

'One . . . Two . . .'

'I couldn't have set Harley up. Believe me, I *couldn't* have.'

'Three, Harry! And figure Four!'

The muzzle of the gun against Harry's neck stirred slightly. There was only a dead man's breath now between Harry Mearns and oblivion.

'*Fi* . . .'

Mearns' bellow was like the detonation of the gun itself.

'. . . because I'M the one working f'r *British* security, Crofts!'

Crofts had already eased the trigger and was staring at Mearns with the sweat of what-had-so-nearly-been now varnishing *his* forehead, by the time Harry Mearns slammed the arm of the chair in bitter frustration.

And snarled, 'Christ, man: it's me – not Eric Harley – who's the good guy. Working to kill the Spearfish hijack FOR the bloody British!'

CHAPTER EIGHTEEN

In a sense Pamela Trevelyan was indirectly responsible for saving Harry Mearns' life. Because even as Harry spat out his outrageous claim, Crofts had asked himself what the hell he was *doing*?

Kill Harry – execute him here in the dying room of Tarvit Farm – and he would place himself outside the law forever. He'd be on the run then, not as a falsely-accused innocent but as a guilty murderer. And that would mean the end of any prospects of seeing Pamela again, and retiring from his nightmares.

'So you're working for British Intelligence, eh, Harry?'

'Yeah! Which means you c'n take the bloody gun away, you bastard!' Harry was breathing a little more freely, now.

Crofts still held the gun.

'You've just claimed that some anonymous Mister Big is prepared to share what could be a lot of money with you . . .'

'A lot of money,' Mearns confirmed with relish, momentarily showing a flash of his old ebullience.

'Yet you're also telling me that you suddenly got patriotic: felt compelled to give up all that loot for the sake of your country. *You*, Harry? No way.'

'Did I *say* I was being a bloody philanthropist?' Mearns squirmed irritably. 'I just went to the market place. Volunteered my services to British Intelligence as an undercover man: offered to double-cross Andersen's crowd for fifty thousand, sterling. To me a bird in the hand was worth two in a dodgy torpedo hijack.'

That was the moment when Crofts did ease the gun and,

for the first time, believed he might have gained an unexpected ally after all. Because that *was* a credible motive;
much more typical of the Harry Mearns that Crofts had
known and long despised.

He didn't really have a lot of choice at that stage, anyway.

If he wasn't prepared to rely on Mearns, he should have
shot him there and then, because he knew one thing for
certain – that if he let Harry go, and Harry Mearns proved
to have been lying, then Harry would turn and kill *him* with
as little compunction as Scarred-Hand had shown to the
two policemen.

There were still questions, though.

'Why allow the hijack to get this far? Why, if you've
tipped them off, haven't British Security already arrested
Andersen while *Marauder*'s still berthed in Oban, Harry?'

Mearns shrugged, wryly massaging the back of his neck.
'There's more to it than that. Doing it your way, the Brits
don't need to pay *me* fifty grand. They want the Mole as
well.'

'The Mole?'

'Somebody in the Ministry of Defence has to be leaking
information about the Spearfish delivery schedules to
Andersen. Probably the same guy who dreamed up the
heist; who stands to gain as Mister Big. Either way, the
Naval security boys have set a trap . . . the movement order
for sea delivery of the weapon has been changed, and its new
routing leaked only to a few suspects. That way, when the
attack takes place they'll be able to eliminate all but the
guilty man – the Mole.'

'Which means they're taking a helluva risk. They'll have
to wait until the last minute,' Crofts breathed. 'It's the only
way they'll have positive proof the revised skeds were
passed.'

'All the way to the brink, Major: let the attack actually
start, then hit them from behind. That's where I'm supposed
to come in . . . and while that's happening, internal security
will be watching their own suspects in the Ministry of

Defence. Waiting for whoever is the rotten apple to betray his hand.'

Crofts chewed his lip. It was all beginning to add up. Simpson himself had confirmed that there was an undercover agent within the Tarvit team – only he'd appeared to believe it was Eric Harley. But say he'd made an error of identity? Alternatively, assuming Simpson himself was the MOD mole – but planning a purely criminal operation as Harry claimed – then he would have had an even more personal motive for eliminating anyone working against the hijack . . .

'Where do Mulders and the other two fit in?'

'Harley an' me were to move aboard the ship for the actual operation. Them boys was recruited as muscle and to position the leading lights for the night entry.' Mearns grinned sardonically; the familiar, callous Harry. 'I could've hired wooden posts with as much intelligence, but it's academic anyway – *Marauder*'s never goin' to get as far as Quarry Cove tomorrow night.'

'So the hit *is* planned for tomorrow.'

'Zero two hundred hours: twelve miles off the coast. The trials Spearfish is being brought to Ardarroch by sea: an unarmed range auxiliary vessel, would you believe?'

'And after the hijack, then what?'

'*Marauder* runs into the cove at high-speed – timing's the essence at that stage. She off-loads Spearfish and heads straight back out to the open sea. They're going to abandon her then, in the Gemini; blow her up just to confuse the issue. Simultaneously, the torpedo's to be flown out by private plane before the security forces have time to react.'

He couldn't help wondering if Mearns really would have gunned Eric down with the others aboard *Marauder* at the critical moment. Though Eric had appreciated the rules of the mercenary game; had always taken chances with his eyes open. What was it they said? – if you go hunt with the vultures, you risk getting shot with the vultures.

He shrugged. 'You'll earn your fifty grand: it's a bloody long shot. It all hangs on your being able to take out seven, maybe eight or nine of *Marauder*'s crew by surprise: stop them before they actually make the attack.'

'Correction. On *our* being able to stop them, Crofts.'

'Our?'

Mearns bowed mockingly. 'I'm only a sergeant major. I need an officer to lead me. Sir.'

Crofts already felt the old familiar butterfly of pre-action nerves stirring in his gut. It was a good feeling this time, though: he wanted Scarred-Hand so badly he could taste the hate. If anything would convince him Harry Mearns was on the level it was that. For him to be invited to attend the final act.

'You want to smuggle me aboard *Marauder*?'

'I warned you you were getting yourself in deep. You've just volunteered yourself back in the killing game again, Crofts. It'll be like the old days, when we hit Scar-Hand Andersen and his bully boys from behind.'

That look was there once more in Harry Mearns' eyes; the distant, hooded look. Crazy Harry Mearns, savouring as ever the eve of bloody violence. Or was it so, this time? Wasn't there something more? Could it have been irony – or simmering resentment?

'After all those years in the wilderness, Crofts. Who'd have guessed the time would ever come f'r degenerates like us to fight for our own beloved country?'

Crofts prowled back and forth within an unlit room, hidden from prying eyes for a large part of that interminable waiting day.

He did other things too, in preparation. Mearns offered him the choice of weapons from an armoury concealed within the old barn – a deliberately random selection as he'd already observed in the hands of the Woollen Men: no common factor to help trace them back. Crofts finally settled for a nine-mil Israeli Uzi with a folding metal stock, one 40-round staggered magazine for ready use and one spare clip of twenty-five. There wasn't a lot of point in weighting himself with more. The cyclic rate of fire of a Uzi submachine gun was 650 rounds per minute but Crofts had always been a realist. He'd watched those Scandinavian mercenaries work as a team and reckoned the advantage of surprise might just earn him the chance to make, maybe, one mag change before Andersen's crowd were eliminated. Or, alternatively, before he and Mearns were.

Crofts cleaned the Uzi with infinite care before he slept. And then woke up in the middle of the night, and cleaned the gun again.

He had another nightmare, too. About Hermann Bosche. But this one had been different; had afforded much broader scope for the melancholia trapped within his mind. Oh, he was holding the Beretta as ever, with Troop Sergeant Bosche's glazing stare focussing on the muzzle; bloodied lips moving in mute appeal; the same wavering backcloth of severed legs and heads and human offal; his finger trembling, locked within the trigger guard and unable to depress . . . but then, suddenly, Bosche had become Eric *Harley*! And Crofts had actually heard Eric screaming his agonised plea, only this time the plea had been for mercy, not for death. And lo and behold he, Crofts, had begun to cry tears of joy because all of a sudden he'd learned why his hesitation had been justified: now he could let Eric live instead of die under the Beretta. Until, just as his nightmare was fighting to become a dream he'd suddenly found another finger upon his – a bleached, corpse-white finger. And *it* had begun to squeeze even though Crofts was desperately trying to save Eric Harley's life.

And then, perhaps, had come the most awful part of all. For just as the gun kicked back, detonated under the relentless pressure of that macabre white finger, Eric's features had also changed . . . to those of Pam Trevelyan! And Crofts had awakened with bulging eyes still retaining a hideous image – of whirling golden hair drenched in blood, and flying white-bone splinters where once had been exquisite flesh, and parted crimson lips and ivory teeth exploding in a bloodied, mish-mash flower of ultimate horror . . .

Oh dear Jesus CHRIIIIIST!

Harry went out on the farm in the morning, trailing his two remaining Boers in desultory search for good, honest agricultural labour. Should the police be watching, they had to be seen to be working as near normally as any farmhands would in the circumstances. Crofts watched them from the window without sympathy. He could see the other two were sick nervous; Mulders' killing had undermined any morale they'd ever had. He didn't think, when they came to arrest them at Quarry Cove after the job was blown, that there would be too much fight from Harry's leading lights.

He talked a lot to Laura, too: trying to persuade her that Den of Tarvit Farm was not a place in which to stay that coming night. There wasn't any good reason for his caution – *Marauder* would never reach the coast whatever happened; alive or not by then, Mearns and he would certainly have aborted that part of the hijack. The only strangers to Tarvit should be the security forces themselves, calling to collect Harry's boys when they tidied up the pieces.

Then why did Crofts feel such a deep unease? Was it simply because of Laura's own tightly-contained suffering? She'd been strangely hardened ever since she'd surprised him in his Tartan Shop refuge: not with the strained sadness of bereavement, though that was certainly there, but rather a continuing detachment; a grimness of purpose – the same ice-cold determination to avenge Eric's murder she'd shown earlier.

The last thing Crofts did before he left her alone at Tarvit on that final evening of the Auchenzie affair was to place his own gun on the kitchen table beside her. He knew she wouldn't need it, probably wouldn't be able to bring herself to fire it anyway ... but it still held four Parabellum dum-dum rounds, and that surely had to afford some small comfort to anyone, even a woman, under fear. Certainly Crofts wouldn't need his old metallic friend on this operation – the Uzi's six-fifty shots per minute offered a greater prospect of his walking away from the confined shipbound killing ground he was heading for.

She'd taken it, and smiled faintly, and then kissed him. Impersonally though, only the faintest butterfly wings of lips almost absently brushing his cheek as he stepped from that sad little house. He knew then she could never love him, but that didn't seem to matter anymore. Not now. Not when she didn't even attempt to prevent his going.

There was one further reason for Crofts' disquiet, but that was even more intangible: based not so much on what was to come as on what had already passed. It wouldn't stop running through his head; over and over again as the two of them drove warily back towards Oban, and *Marauder*.

It all revolved around Harry Mearns' earlier comment. That bit about, '. . . after all those years in the wilderness, Crofts. Who'd have guessed the time would ever come f'r degenerates like us to fight for our own beloved country'!

You see, Crofts had easily understood, maybe even subscribed to the sarcasm. And been captured himself by the sense of irony. But one particular aspect *had* seemed odd, and not a little disturbing.

The way Harry Mearns had literally spat out that word *Beloved*!

CHAPTER NINETEEN

The oil supply ship had already sailed from her berth when Crofts and Mearns arrived, and with her had gone her lights. *Marauder* now lay cocooned in a private darkness; a silent, unwelcoming hull with only occasional reflections to break the ragged confusion of gear about her deck.

There was one man on watch, casually awaiting Mearns' arrival. The move out must be seen as a routine sailing; the departure of a survey vessel about her daily work. No one would raise a curious eyebrow in Oban, where vessels constantly called and then moved on. Anyway, by normal standards, if the hijack *had* been compromised then any state of alert on the Woollen Men's part would have proved inadequate; the British security forces would descend in force and the game be up irrespective.

Crofts hovered in the shadows until Mearns and the sentry stepped inside the accommodation, then shinned gently down the quayside ladder and on to the deck. Silently he moved to the after end, the still-folded Uzi nestling in the crook of his right arm, already cocked and set to 'Automatic'. He'd passed the point of no return; if he was surprised, then someone was going to die irrespective. He hoped that if anyone came upon him here, it would be Scarred-Hand himself.

Half way along the deck something rattled. Crofts hesitated: listening. A vagrant breeze played upon his blackened face, for Crofts was already wearing the camouflage of night war. The curious rattle came again. Close by. Carefully he moved towards the semi-rigid inflatable secured in chocks along the starboard side, eyes narrowed, finger caressing the trigger.

The whisp of wind once more, curling round the dripping, weed-dank piers; fluttering the canvas cover of the rubber craft . . . and Crofts relaxed expressionlessly. A lanyard had been carelessly left unsecured on the cover itself: flapping regularly as the breeze undulated along the faded orange material.

He slipped further aft again, a shadow within the shadows, peering in search of the one hiding place Harry had assured him would be safe – and then he saw it. Please God it wasn't locked . . . but as Mearns had predicted, it was open. Quickly he raised the hatch and slid down the vertical ladder within. The smell of paint and sea-bilge and hydraulic oil enveloped him as he replaced the hatch above him, then triggered the shaded torch he'd carried, dimly illuminating the tiny compartment designated as his temporary sanctuary.

It was *Marauder*'s tiller flat: the space containing her steering gear. Verdigreased and salt-encrusted copper pipes sketched a hydraulic web towards the friction-shiny rams; rusted quadrants poised above her twin rudders awaiting guidance from a helmsman's hand upon her wheel; a clutch of mouldering paint pots; a broken deck scrubber. It was quiet down there with only the lap of water against her outer skin and the muffled creak of mooring lines as she stirred gently against her berth.

Very quiet. As quiet as . . . a grave?

He lit a Lucky Strike, settled down and unfolded the Uzi stock; casually covering the hatch above. Crofts was very calm; his nerves had settled as they always did once he was committed. All he could do now was wait.

The engine started with a shudder just before midnight, first port and then starboard exhausts exploding with distant roars before settling to a steady grumble of throttled-back power. Simultaneously the quadrants began to turn, creaking under their hydraulic beckoning; hard to starboard, hard to port, testing all was well.

Crofts listened alertly to the sounds of a vessel preparing to slip. A bang on deck, directly above his head; the clatter of boots, the shuffling slide of a wire being dragged inboard, then another rattle of lines snaking through fairleads . . . the quadrants hissed, began to swing as the port engine increased its throaty growl. Under him the hull shivered and began to bounce rhythmically as the prop turned slow astern, springing *Marauder* away from the quayside itself.

Then a momentary lull as the engine died; only the frantic splash of wavelets atomising against her moving counter as she slid from the dock. Quadrants swinging again, clawing her head to port . . . and then the turbo-charged rumble of her engines gradually increasing as she headed out across Oban Bay and into the secret night.

Crofts settled back and tried to ignore the motion. He'd never had much to do with boats. Down here, particularly in the darkness of the tiller flat, with the shipboard stench of bilge and oil and tar, the constant hiss of the steering gear and the clank of unseen things, he felt a fish out of water . . . Correction – a soldier *on* the bloody water!

He concentrated on thinking about Mearns, about what Mearns might be doing right then, and how far he could trust Mearns anyway.

It hadn't been practical to plan any precise strategy for taking out Andersen's crew; events would turn on where Mearns found himself when they closed with the target vessel. The *Marauder* complement would be under briefing now for the parts they had to play and, unless Mearns could find a safe way of communication before the hijack, Crofts had no option but to stay below until he detected the manoeuvring which would indicate that the attack was imminent.

Their understanding was that Crofts was to take the initiative: Crofts would fire first, the only warning Harry might get . . . and then it had to be 'targets of opportunity'. Hell, it should still work; Mearns had originally intended to take them out all by himself, and had stood a pretty good chance at that, aided by the advantage of surprise. Now there were two of them, and they'd fought through off-the-cuff situations such as this before – interacting as an experienced combat team, each reading the other's intentions in what, so far, had always proved deadly collusion: snap-shooting anything and everything that moved or screamed or simply froze with terror . . .

It *should* still work – as long as Crofts could still trust Harry.

And if not? If Crofts did find himself out there on that lonely after deck with one gun in his hand and up to nine automatic weapons swinging against him, but no Harry Mearns to give him support . . .?

It was one-fifteen: three quarters of an hour to the moment of truth. Crofts lit another cigarette with rapidly diminishing enthusiasm and hunched – chilled to the bone both by the sea-cold and his own increasingly black thoughts – within that swaying, rumbling, foetid crypt.

Twenty minutes later Crofts finally was sea-sick. The motion of the ship had increased severely as the steering gear had sighed and he'd sensed her coming to another course. He rolled over and retched agonisingly into the bilges, praying they would soon be there and this passive misery might vanish under the adrenalin-pulse of action. He tried to exercise his mind, to interlock more of the random pieces of the Auchenzie jigsaw puzzle.

Take the death of the allegedly homosexual Ministry of Defence scientist Thomson, for instance – could that really have had any significance in the Spearfish affair as Eric's drunken ramblings had suggested? If so – what?

And, again assuming Simpson was the Mole, then it still hadn't been explained why Simpson had encouraged him, Crofts, to Den of Tarvit in the first place.

Harry Mearns, Crofts reflected in the throes of his nausea, always had been able to present a thoroughly logical argument, as long as the listener didn't feel bound to confuse practicality with morality . . . but was Harry really telling the whole truth?

It seemed a long time before *Marauder*'s engines finally throttled to a growl, and the violent motion subsided to a steady see-saw roll. Crofts crouched with the Uzi at the ready, listening intently; any thought of seasickness already forgotten.

He sensed that all the speculation, all the waiting, all the running which he'd done since he'd come to Den of Tarvit Farm was finally over.

The blued muzzle of the submachine gun came out of the steering flat hatch first. Then Crofts followed, sliding over the coaming and immediately rolling prone along the deck facing forward, the Uzi trained to cover *Marauder*'s faintly silhouetted bridge.

It was pitch dark, the wind tugging and flailing at his hair, the ghostly phosphorescence of the bow wave sighing astern on either side, flaring and smashing from under the distant bows as the night ship coasted through an otherwise tar-black sea. A perfect time for sinister things, and for men to move in nefarious ways.

There *was* another ship out there – steaming on a roughly parallel course and some fifty metres to starboard. It was hard to make out detail from where Crofts lay, but she appeared to be of a similar type to themselves: long and low, with a Spartan windswept open bridge well forward of a clear afterdeck. Some form of coastal minesweeper perhaps; now converted to Fleet Auxiliary work. There were many specialist craft operated for the Royal Navy by civilian crews: supply ships; oilers; salvage, buoy and boom defence craft. Crofts wasn't a seaman. He didn't have to be; this task was strictly military.

He lay for a few moments longer, watching the vessel opposite. She was still steering a steady course, making no attempt to shy away from her nocturnal visitor. It seemed odd to Crofts at first; that she was taking no avoiding action. Surely the knowledge of her high risk cargo should have made her officers wary: an anonymous ship like *Marauder* closing with her in the middle of the night?

But then again, they'd been given no cause for mistrust, for wasn't that the essence of the counter-intelligence trap? That nobody engaged in the thinking torpedo project – not even the crew of the actual target vessel – *were* to be warned of the proposed hijack: only told that a last minute alteration had been made to the delivery vessel's route?

Suddenly an Aldis signalling lamp flashed from the ship across the water. And Crofts discovered why the Auxiliary carrying Spearfish was prepared to slow, even reluctantly. His lips moved soundlessly as he read the flickering light:

THIS IS AN MOD CLASSIFIED SUPPLY MOVE. MY ORDERS ARE TO MAINTAIN RADIO SILENCE OTHER THAN FOR PURPOSES OF SAFE NAVIGATION. I ACCEPT HM CUSTOMS INSPECTION ONLY UNDER STRONGEST PROTEST AND INTEND TO REPORT MATTER TO MARITIME HQ ON DOCKING.

So *that* was how Scarred-Hand had managed it. Without a word being passed on radio! He'd gambled on their not being prepared to transmit a formal inter-service complaint on an open channel while still at sea. He'd also guessed shrewdly that no demand from an assumed Revenue cutter for boarding facilities could be totally ignored by a civilian-manned Fleet Auxiliary. Her Majesty's Customs and Excise still retained the authority to stop and search any vessel within United Kingdom waters. Maybe the master of that ship over there was even looking forward to addressing a few choice seaman-to-civil-servant words to any over-zealous bloody Exciseman who might step aboard.

Crofts tensed. It was beginning to happen; figures were moving aft at last. Three men; one moving ponderously under some bulky form of back pack still unidentifiable through the darkness. Silently he drew back, rolling under the cover of the inflatable craft; swivelling the muzzle of the Uzi until it was laid squarely on the centre figure of the three. He was frowning now: peering with uncertain gaze at the equipment carried by that particular mercenary. It was vaguely familiar in silhouette. Hadn't he seen something similar somewhere before; on some distant battlefield? Many years ago . . .

And then he recognised it for what it was. And for the horror it contained.

A flame thrower! Ex-US Army – Model M1 or was it

M1A . . . Christ, who the hell *cared*! All Crofts needed to know was that the weapon the hijacker was carrying could spray eighteen litres of blazing liquid jelly across a thirty yard gap. And that one ten-second burst would clear every living creature from the target's open bridge.

Crofts didn't wait a moment longer. The risk to those sickeningly vulnerable seamen across there was too great. He began to squirm from under the inflatable; pull the butt of the submachine gun harder into his shoulder. Backsight, foresight carefully laid on the bastard preparing his chemical massacre – an' jus' pray to God Harry Mearns is ready as well.

. . . but then, unexpectedly, Crofts himself froze, the breath locking in his throat with the shock of it.

Because that was the moment when the point of a very sharp instrument was placed below his shoulder blade and depressed gently but expertly: just enough to break the skin without actually entering the flesh. Poised where it would kill him with one sharp thrust . . . while, simultaneously, a languid whisper was heard beside his startled ear.

'No conversation; no sudden movement, old boy. Please.'

Now Crofts certainly knew that voice. Oh, Crofts didn't have any difficulty at all in remembering *that* particular voice from the more violent reaches of his past.

The voice added, almost as a suggestion, 'Let's just allow the professionals to get on with what they're being paid a rather large price to accomplish, shall we?'

The voice of Commander Simpson. Commander Edward Simpson, that was. Royal Navy.

And now – or so it would appear – quite *definitely* 'Retired'!

CHAPTER TWENTY

Perhaps Crofts could have tried to warn those unsuspecting seamen. It was unlikely that he would have succeeded. Simpson had already proved himself a master in murder; a most accomplished assassin. He could have killed Crofts so quickly, so silently and so efficiently that not even the three men grouped around that flame thrower less than a choking cry away would have heard his sacrifice.

All Crofts actually did was to huddle helplessly, safely concealed by *Marauder*'s inflatable, in the needle-sharp company of a man now dressed in sensible combat fatigues, who looked very much more like the Mekong Delta pirate Crofts had first met a long time ago, when Eric Harley and two policemen, and a certain Boer Mulders, were still alive.

He could only stare with jaw set tight while Simpson slid his Uzi submachine gun out of harm's way; thereby establishing, as he'd done once before with a Vietnamese sampan, that the sophisticated technology of the Twentieth Century didn't necessarily confer superiority on its possessor.

Simpson sounded just a little disappointed, all the same.

'Much as I'd like to be in on things, we won't distract Andersen – Scarred-Hand, I believe you call him, old boy – right now.'

Crofts watched as the two vessels slowed together and closed until, even through the darkness of that terrible night at sea, Crofts could discern the silhouettes of men clustering on the Auxiliary's open bridge while two more hurried along her decks with fenders at the ready.

Suddenly a searchlight snapped to life from *Marauder*'s

own bridge, blinding the other ship; causing her already angered officers to shield their eyes and curse ... and incidentally, to fail to recognise *Marauder* for what she was.

A voice bellowed from across the narrowing gap: a Scottish voice with a seaman's snap. 'Put yon bluidy LIGHT out, ye daft bastard!'

Closer now, and closer. Forty metres ... thirty ...

Beside Crofts, Simpson stirred warningly. The point of the knife drew a little more blood. 'Don't, old boy. If you want to live long enough to have a chat about it all later.'

Twenty metres ... fifteen ...

Crofts hollowed eyes actually saw it then – Spearfish! A white, cylindrical form banded in green and blue with red warning decals beside its space-age tail; barely bigger than a man, sitting mute in a lifting cradle on the transport vessel's afterdeck; gleaming softly under the glare of the searchlight. An innocuous looking object, with only its thirty-one transducer eyes to reveal any hint of the malevolence programmed within its brain. But at least it had no conception of good or evil; no capability for sensing that its actions were right or wrong.

So it had to be an improvement on men like Simpson and Scarred-Hand in some small measure.

Twelve metres.

'Stop engines!' The sharp, measured command clearly heard now. Then, 'Put yon bluidy LIGHT OUT, Mister!'

The three men on the deck before them were being reinforced. Crofts could see another pair moving surreptitiously to the rail, weapons loosely held by their sides, waiting for the moment. Christ, Harry ... where was bloody *Harry*? Or was he still waiting, as arranged, for the first signal from Crofts?

Ten metres. The short seas crashing and exploding between the rapidly closing hulls.

And then it happened.

Crofts heard the *whoosh* of pressurised gelatine; saw the dripping white-hot flame arc-ing over the gap between the ships; caught for one never-to-be-expunged second the widening eyes of the seamen on the Auxiliary's bridge as they stood with heads back and vacant mouths gaping at the heavenly fire descending upon them.

And then the chemical foulness enveloped the staring men, and they began to burn too, and scream, and try for the first agonising moments of their living cremation to escape, flounder from their blazing confinement until fingers and noses and ears and uniform buttons began to melt. After a very short time even the shrieks muted to animal whimpers – and then there were only the flames sweeping the crackling bridge, blanketing unrecognisable, convulsively-jerking forms which, in their turn, soon ceased to move.

And Crofts, who had watched many dreadful things but never with such helpless frustration and self-loathing, was violently sick.

He was fortunate. The support shoot began just as he vomited, and any sounds he made were covered by the racket of other men's deaths. And Commander Edward Simpson was extraordinarily tolerant because he didn't kill Crofts as he might otherwise have felt forced to to. Just for making a noise.

They machine-gunned the two seamen preparing the fenders as they tried to run away. If there were any more men aboard the target ship then Andersen didn't care: she was already stopped, her wheelhouse and bridge an untenable oven, her radio a molten shambles. It didn't matter if some stray engineers survived below: stealing, not murder had been the object of the exercise. And then making a withdrawal; as quickly as possible, and with military precision. Rescue ships would come very soon, the fires must be visible from the mainland itself, while in the meantime *Marauder* had to make her high-speed dash to off-load at Quarry Cove before continuing her feint across the Irish Sea.

And they did move fast, the Woollen Men: swarming over the rails like monkey-pirates, slinging Spearfish, hooking its cradle and hoisting it to *Marauder*'s single davithead. Within minutes the cylindrical stuff of Crofts' Auchenzie nightmare was swinging free and clear while not once was any order given, any voice raised which might betray the

origins of the hijackers to a stunned survivor of the holo-
caust.

'Soon, old boy,' Simpson breathed encouragingly into
Crofts' ear, 'very soon now we can join my associate on the
bridge, and decide what to do with you.'

But there wasn't to be any decision on Crofts' future –
which wouldn't have been hard to predict, anyway – taken
in conjunction with Scarred-Hand. The moment the last
man had leapt back aboard the night ship her twin engines
detonated in an unexpected snarl of power. Instantly the
deck below Crofts reared as the screws bit deep and
Marauder leapt ahead, with rising bows and the white water
smashing and flaring on either side and the wind suddenly a
shrieking, clawing solid thing as two thousand brake horse-
power bulleted her across that red-reflecting sea. And just
for one split second Crofts felt the knife point falter from his
back as even the experienced naval officer Simpson was
caught off guard by the surge of acceleration.

While, to add to the disruption of Commander Simpson's
cool, *that* was the moment when Harry Mearns finally did
arrive . . .

Bloody berserk – and firing from the hip like a crazy man.

It became a madness; a bedlam. Suddenly men were screaming, shouting, shooting. The pair who'd been by the rails
earlier, the two who'd machine-gunned the Auxiliary's
fender men – were cut down in their turn by Harry Mearns
before they'd even time to reply: their weapons were still
rising when a nine-mil burst doubled them over and hurled
guts and blood in a vivid crimson slash across the bulkhead
behind them.

Crofts was already rolling frantically away from Simpson, clawing for the Uzi. Simultaneously a gutteral voice
began bellowing frantic orders from the direction of the
bridge. No more the quiet machinery of discipline now;
there was a suspension of all initiative aboard *Marauder* in
those initial moments of Mearns' rampage; just as he and
Harry had relied on. Only now they'd got exactly what

they'd needed – and Crofts wasn't bloody *ready*!

His grasping hand slapped down on the metal stock of the Israeli weapon, dragged it with him as he continued to roll; fumbling for the plastic trigger grip, to bring it round to fire all in one panicky convulsion. He heard himself roaring '*Harry*! Get this bastard first, Harrrryyyy!'

Abruptly, shockingly, there came a massive explosion from what already seemed a long way astern. The Naval Auxiliary was detonating in a series of rumbling, mushrooming explosions; great leaping tongues of fire soaring to the clouds, breaking away in excited flames licking ever higher as the red sea around her reared and froze in terror. *Christ* but she must've been carrying some form of armament after all, whatever Harry Mearns had said. Or was it more Fleet cargo: ammunition? explosives?

Crofts caught one glimpse of Commander Simpson then; lunging towards him, silhouetted against the inferno in *Marauder*'s skying wake. A black cut-out Dracula of a man rising above him with shapeless combat clothing fluttering in the smash of the wind and the once-colourless eyes now red-reflecting the violence-light with a glittering malevolence.

Plus the knife! Simpson might have selected it as a silent method of killing Crofts had he tried to shout a warning, but now it was proving a cardinal error. Now it was as ill-chosen a threat in that Twentieth Century firefight as a bow and arrow – except to Crofts. To him, it still represented the prospect of extinction long before he could bring *his* particularly six-fifty-shots-a-minute product of modern war to bear.

And then Harry finally saw them. But Harry was still mad as a parrot with Crofts; Harry was bloody *furious*!

'Ohhh, you bastard!' Harry Mearns' features were a mask of contempt. 'You let 'em *do* it, you useless gutless . . .'

Another figure came running round the side of the deckhouse with a blazing Spanish Star submachine gun. Harry casually snap-shot him and the man kept on running through the rails and over into the foaming water, still firing.

'. . . BASTARD!' Harry finished.

'Shuttup an' get *Simpson*!' Crofts bawled.

But Simpson, previously concealed from Mearns, was already swinging desperately, his hand arc-ing back across his shoulder – now clutching the point, not the handle of the knife so urgently diverted from the task of Crofts' demise. Simpson was certain to die and Simpson must have known it . . . but he still reacted to the most immediate threat; still worked like the highly trained pirate he'd been in the service of Her Majesty.

Harry Mearns only got one shot off before the knife crossed the intervening gap. It was enough – Crofts felt Simpson catapult backwards across him and crash to the deck, all hunched and not at all debonair any more; even pathetic, somehow, like a rat kicked by a farmer's boot. Simultaneously he heard Mearns mutter 'Oh, Jesus' in a funny voice and dragged his eyes from Simpson's body to see Harry sitting on the engine room skylight, bent forward at the waist with Simpson's knife protruding from his shoulder.

There wasn't time for any more casual bystanding, though. Scarred-Hand was shouting again from *Marauder*'s bridge and, even as Crofts clawed erect with the Uzi finally at the ready, two more Woollen Men raced from forward, one already shooting, the other presenting a sawn-off shot-gun as he advanced. Crofts heard himself releasing all his pent-up hate in reckless euphoria as he at last stood his ground; the Uzi racketing and shuddering and the cordite smoke acrid and whirling around him before being snatched by the howling winds of *Marauder*'s race.

The two violent men evaporated violently; gory tatters and a stitch of nine millimetre holes an obscene graffiti against the after end of the deckhousing. Crofts began to run towards Mearns just as a Luger automatic, followed by an apprehensive head and a white boiler-suit collar, appeared at the engine room skylight in cautious search for some guide as to what the hell was happening.

Crofts gave him a most explicit hint. He shot him just above the boiler-suit collar. The Luger went skitting along the deck towards Mearns and the engineer went back to his engines.

'How many more f'r . . .'

'Three.' Harry winced, gingerly holding on to the knife. 'Andersen, the wheelman, and one. They're down to you, Major.'

'Easy. Don't pull it out,' Crofts panted, the Uzi barrel nervously scanning from port to starboard for anything that moved. They were hard against the after end of the wheelhouse now, temporarily out of sight of Scarred-Hand, and he was suddenly concerned about Mearns. All said an' done, Harry Mearns had turned up trumps: for the first time in his life Crofts felt an unwilling kinship with the ex-CSM of Column Delta. 'Don't pull the bloody knife out or you'll bleed even faster.'

'Don't,' Harry retorted succinctly, his pain a sweating varnish to his brow, 'be so fucking *stupid*!'

Crofts began to ease himself, submachine gun across his chest, back hard against the bulkhead, around the turn of the wheelhouse. God, it was weird . . . this firefight at thirty knots with the wind still screaming like a banshee and the now untended engines a flat-our roar and the whole ship bucking and leaping and careering across the choppy sea towards the coast which lay ahe . . .

'Mearns,' Crofts asked suddenly, halting again. 'How long did you say this monster takes to get from the hijack position back to Quarry Cove?'

'Not long. Only a few min . . .'

And then it was Mearns' turn to look unhappy as Crofts' meaning struck him too. They must have used up nearly all the time they had left. 'You do *know* how to stop this gallopin' bastard once you've taken Andersen out, don't you?'

Crofts felt a modest gratitude for Harry's confidence. Had he been the one to say it, it would've been: '*if* you took Andersen out'! Nevertheless his nerves were getting frayed to say the least.

'Look, I'm a soldier,' he snarled irritably. 'If I knew anything about boats I'd've joined the Navy in the first bloody place, Mearns.'

'Throttles,' Harry pleaded. 'Up there on the bridge. Like on an aeroplane, Crofts.'

'I can't,' Crofts informed him tightly, 'fly a bloody aeroplane either.'

'You jus' pull 'em back an' . . .'

But then Harry Mearns' concern locked on to something presenting an even more imminent threat – something already happening right behind Crofts – and his already ashen lips contorted half in terror, half in outrage. 'Crofts! Look OUT, Crofts!'

Crofts was already swinging though, taking up first pressure on the Uzi, hearing and instantly recognising the *hiss* of pressurised air even as he registered the bulky shape rising from the deck with the twin tanks harnessed to his back.

And the nozzle of that flame thrower laid directly on them. Already dripping the first white-hot globules of primary fire.

The Israeli Uzi submachine gun has a muzzle velocity of over thirteen hundred feet per second, expending an 8-gram Parabellum round. Crofts fired quite a number of them in the split seconds he and Mearns had left to earn survival. And he was shooting at point blank range, which makes for a highly penetrative group.

They must have tunnelled clear through the Woollen Man with the flamethrower, and continued into the tanks of nightmare gel strapped firmly to his back. Fortunately the impact also slammed him astern and clear of Crofts and Mearns.

Just before he, quite simply, blew up. Exploded. Like a human Roman Candle; in a great white flash and a ball of circulating fire and a hideous shrapnel of Things.

Crofts flinched, gaping; shaken to the core until Mearns roared, 'Go, Major . . . GO!' And that was when Crofts knew that if he didn't now, then he never would – and hurled himself round the corner of the deckhousing with the sick fear bitter in his throat, racing towards *Marauder*'s starboard bridge ladder through the spray-lash of her juggernaut progress.

Only two Woollen Men left. One was already at the head of the ladder, frozen, staring astern in open-mouthed shock as the funeral pyre of his comrade billowed in raging liquid fire; spilling along the afterdeck; trickling in Vesuvius torrents down her sides; igniting the fabric of the ship; flickering and reaching for the pristine white cylinder that was the partly-loaded Spearfish torpedo still dangling from the davit.

The *torpedo*!

With an oven below. And no way of knowing whether it was already fitted with an explosive warhead for its trials role.

Crofts shot the second-last mercenary at the top of the ladder economically. One round only, cleanly through the head. He wanted to save what few he must have left for the last and most dearly wanted Woollen Man of all. Crofts, too, was temporarily insane by then; berserk at what they were forcing him to do and at what they and Simpson had already done to Laura Harley.

The crewman plummetted down the ladder in a flail of bloodied arms and legs. Crofts didn't wait: he kept on clawing his way up the tumbling man, stamping and sliding over the corpse, spurred on by the terrible careless rage within him. And it *was* a foolishness of anger; even as he burst upon that open bridge his madness evaporated, he became aware of his own mortality again. Scarred-Hand could kill him easily now, exposed and vulnerable as he'd left himself in his final unthinking assault.

Only the bullets never came. And yet again Crofts hesitated fractionally because too many things had taken place already which made no sense; and this time it seemed terribly important to try and understand why.

It was very dark up there, eyes still blinded by the flash of the firebomb man, but gradually he discerned the tall figure of Andersen standing calmly before the wheel of *Marauder*. Only Andersen didn't seem to care about his presence – just stood there, staring straight ahead, with the slipstream flaying his handsome blond hair into whirling streamers and his hands – the hideously disfigured hands that first marked him – delicately caressing the bucking wheel with the love that only a seaman could hold for a ship.

Finally Andersen did turn his face towards Crofts, and smiled the mocking smile that Crofts had only seen previously through a black-wool hood. And said with that same careful yet alien precision, 'So it is over, Major Crofts. Everything is over.'

Crofts still didn't understand, but he read Andersen's eyes then. Dimly, through the night. They held the same wistful regret as had the eyes of Troop Sergeant Bosche. Regret for things unfinished, life as yet unlived, and glorious victories suddenly an unattainable dream . . .

There could be no more hesitation.

He said, 'Not quite,' and shot Andersen; a vertical burst beginning at the lower abdomen and stitching upwards. It was a dreadful, savage way to kill any kind of man. Still, when the fortieth expended cartridge had tinkled to the deck and the Uzi fell silent because its magazine was finally empty, there was no Scarred-Hand anymore; no hate; no feeling. Only a glistening trail leading back across the tiny bridge and out into the spindrift darkness.

Crofts stood for a moment, drained. Slowly he turned forward, staring sightlessly ahead at first, thrusting his face above the glass screen and reaching desperately for the anaesthetising blast of that keening, buffeting tornado marking the runaway *Marauder*'s progress.

Until, suddenly, his eyes opened wider.

Because Crofts understood, then, what Scarred-Hand had meant when he'd said, with such wistful certainty, 'everything is over . . .'

There were two red lights directly in front of him: one above the other. Leading lights. Just like one would have expected at Quarry Cove. There was also the black loom of cliffs reaching almost – or so it appeared to Crofts' now hypnotised gaze – to the scudding clouds themselves, while below *them* was a faint line of white which could only be the seas breaking thunderously against the granite base of Quarry Pier. By any standards, *Marauder*'s arrival had to be considered a perfect landfall.

. . . except that Quarry Pier was now less than half a minute's passage time ahead.

And the pirate ship *Marauder* weighed well in excess of a hundred tons. She was still travelling at full turbo-charged revolutions – at over thirty knots. There wasn't any time to try and turn her while, even for an experienced seaman like Simpson, attempting to slow her down in those final moments could only have proved a futile and panic-stricken measure.

Crofts, now in sole command, didn't panic. Good Lord, no.

F'r a start, he didn't even know where the bloody throttles WERE!

CHAPTER TWENTY-ONE

When Andersen's ship did finally terminate her bloody voyage at Den of Tarvit Farm, it was as a stone skimmed across the surface of a pond.

Without a final helm correction she hit the extreme ledge of the seaward reef first; the largely submerged shelf of rock guarding the entrance to Quarry Cove. *Marauder* took off then, rearing and bounding from the sea like some monstrous breaching whale with the water streaming behind her and the shriek of her still-spinning shafts a gargantuan requiem. Already her keel had been stripped away; her intestines opened to the night. In that split second she was a ship no longer; she was a flying machine, but without the means of flight.

Crofts found himself slammed prone as the bridgedeck rose beneath him: screwing his red-rimmed eyes tight shut, curling into a foetal ball with his hands clamped terror-stricken around his head. He was conscious only of a befuddled awareness of his own propensity for disaster. Every responsibility in the Spearfish nightmare had been placed on him. Even now, Andersen's chilling acceptance of the price of failure; his so-acquiescent suicide by default under Crofts' gun . . . even that had been turned against him. His first command at sea – and after less than one minute, look what he'd managed to bloody *do* to it!

Marauder pancaked next on the jumbled granite teeth of Quarry Pier with Behemoth inertia, exploding the belly out of her, spewing forth tons of engine and fuel tanks and ballast and pipework, catapulting boat and deck fittings and corpses and pieces of still burning things in a vast shower of sparks whirling up towards the lowering sky; obliterating the ancient crane with the brand new lifting wire that had provided the first hint of villainy afoot; causing a thousand sleeping seabirds to awake and scatter their wheeling, squawking terror abroad on the sea.

She rose again in her avalanching agony but more wearily now. A dying convulsion. Something heavy fell back aboard her with a crash and lodged across her bridge, directly above Crofts. He didn't dare open his eyes; just cowered even more tightly in his private hell-hole until he felt her bone-jar final grounding. This time there was salt water and spray and a sudden hysterical terror of drowning. Immediately she began to fall starboard and Crofts could numbly detect the roar of ingressing sea.

He opened his eyes and blinked up at the sky, and saw the long white ghost balanced above him. Only it wasn't a ghost, it was the torpedo, Spearfish, the cause of his being here. Torn violently from the davithead it lay broken now; dented and scarred, its thirty-one glinting electronic eyes staring malevolently down upon him from the ruptured nosecone. Just for one fleeting, fanciful moment Crofts honestly did imagine he'd surprised it while it was 'thinking'.

Or might it have been simply . . . laughing?

Marauder fell further over on her side and water began to rush towards the head of the ladder.

Crofts dragged himself to his feet and began to search for Harry Mearns.

He managed to drag Mearns ashore. Harry had also survived somehow: still clinging to the engine room hatch with his one good arm and swearing like a company sergeant major. Oh, Harry Mearns had proved himself indestructible all right, but he would still be in Crofts' debt — Crofts grinned to himself at that: Harry would really hate that prospect — because Harry could never have made it to the beach at Quarry Cove without Crofts, not with that knife of Simpson's still spitted through his shoulder.

They collapsed in the shingle at the foot of the cliff path

for a few minutes; breathing stertorously and watching Marauder's final dying. She didn't sink completely, the water was too shallow within the inner harbour where her aeronautical cruise had ultimately crash-landed her. Now she lay on her side with the fires almost quenched on her afterdeck, the cleansing water reaching half way up her bloodied, bullet-scarred decks, and things still rolling and tumbling to the cove. A body floating towards the beach, face down with arms and legs in crucifix, and then the semi-rigid inflatable, collapsed and riddled with bullet holes, under which Crofts and Simpson had spent some little time together.

It was a pity about Simpson. There were still too many answers dying with Marauder. Crofts would desperately have liked to have enjoyed a few more words with Commander bloody Simpson before Harry had been forced to kill him.

Mearns finally stirred and grunted. 'I'm going up the path to the top.'

Crofts didn't take his eyes from Marauder. 'It's all right, Harry. They'll come for us now. They must've seen the fires.'

Well, there wasn't a lot of point in running any longer. It was ended. Crofts had won his innocence: Crofts was even a sort of hero. Crofts and Harry were even sorts of heroes.

'I said I'm going up that bloody path!' Harry Mearns snapped, unexpectedly petulant.

Crofts did look at Harry then. A bit put out. Well Christ, but hadn't he just saved Harry's life? An' what was the gain in punishing themselves further now it was all over?

But then Crofts found that it wasn't over at all. That as far as Harry Mearns was concerned, it seemed it never had been. Because Mearns now held a Luger automatic trained on Crofts' chest – the same gun which had skittered from the hand of the boiler-suited engineer shot by Crofts through the skylight – and Mearns very obviously intended to use it.

Right then.

'Maybe you didn't hear me right, Major. I didn't say

"we" were going to the top of the cliffs: I said *I* was.'

Harry Mearns did smile fractionally at that, but it was a humourless grin. Perhaps revealing even the faintest touch of regret.

'You won't be goin' anywhere, Crofts. Y'see – you'll be dead.'

There wasn't time for disbelief. Crofts had a cold feeling there wasn't a lot of time for anything.

'Is this you squaring the books because I held a gun to your head, Harry?' he asked, forcing his voice to stay calm. 'If it is, then f'r God's sake remember – I didn't pull the trigger.'

'Christ, it isn't *that*: it's nothing personal at all,' Harry assured him consolingly. 'This is strictly business, Crofts.'

Crofts shook his head determinedly. 'Oh, no. No, you owe me, Harry. I pulled you off that wreck – you owe me too much to do that, whatever crazy reasons you have.'

Harry began to get up, wincing. The gun lifted until it was lined on Crofts' head. 'I warned you at the start you were getting in too deep. It's a stinkin' game. There's no rules for collecting debts. I can't afford to risk paying mine.'

'All right! So if you're going to, then an explanation first won't cost you much,' Crofts pressed him urgently. 'Everyone's given some reason for his own execution, Harry – you can afford to give me that much.'

Mearns hesitated, hunched irresolutely in the darkness. It was the first hint of uncertainty.

'Twenty years, Harry.' Crofts added tensely. 'Like each other or not, we've fought alongside each other for nearly twenty years. Another few minutes – a few words to tell me why?'

They were the longest few seconds Crofts had ever lived through. But at least he did live through them. Eventually Mearns shrugged. 'O.K., so we walk a while first – but stay ahead of me, Major: well ahead. Otherwise you won't hear any words: you won't even hear the bullet.'

They began to stumble forward in the fading light of *Marauder*'s fires. Crofts led the way as ordered; eyes all the time probing the blackness at the top of that short cliff. Surely to God someone was around; some of the alerted security forces. Hell, they knew that Harry's boys would be there. Though come to that, where *were* Harry's boys?

'Probably gone,' Harry called sardonically, as if reading his mind. 'You think a couple of drop-outs like them would hang around after what's happened? I'm even surprised they stayed long enough to mount the lights – we must've looked like a runaway express train comin' in.'

Crofts clambered a few steps higher then gave up searching for policemen. He'd guessed by then that they never had been waiting at the top. It was his own fault: he should've listened to his own suspicions earlier. Mearns had virtually betrayed himself right at the beginning. When he'd poured such contempt into the phrase '. . . beloved country!'

'You never were working for British Intelligence were you, Harry? So tell me – how long have you been a bloody Russian agent?'

'Ohhh, about twenty years,' Harry said matter-of-factly.

Crofts slowed abruptly. Twenty *years*? Ever since his court-martial? All those old suspicions flooded back – the unexplained ambushes; the mercenary operations anticipated before they'd even entered the field; targets evaporating just before they hit them. The betrayal of Column Delta, which had also destroyed Troop Sergeant Bosche . . . the Soviets must have paid Harry a lot over twenty years of treason.

'Move, Crofts!' Mearns snapped. 'Your time's precious: don't waste it on moral indignation. We all did it f'r the money – you, me, Harley, Simpson . . . especially Simpson; hiding behind his oath of allegiance to Queen and Country. I'm no more a dedicated Commie than you are. "Mercenary", Crofts, that's the name of our game; an' there's no damn difference between Andersen's rednecks aboard *Marauder* an' the true blue, holier-than-thou guys like you – except maybe a larger dose of hypocrisy.'

And maybe, just maybe, Harry Mearns wasn't entirely wrong at that.

They were half way up the path now. The sea wind was rising, tugging at Crofts' plastered wet hair, moaning against the rock faces around them. As Mearns had promised, time was running out. Crofts kept climbing, calling against the wind.

'Simpson even warned me it was a Soviet operation in Oban. Why did he do that when he was one of you, Harry?'

'He wasn't. He made up that particular espionage story to cover his own motives,' Harry laughed cynically. 'He was a damn sight closer to the truth than he realised.'

'Then he, at least, *did* intend to blackmail the Brits over the torpedo? He was more a business man than a traitor?'

'He'd become disenchanted with the Royal Navy after Nam, Crofts: he'd worked all his life for them and they'd passed him over for promotion. That was when he decided to capitalise on his access to Top Secret information and turn it to personal profit.'

'So he came to you with the idea for a criminal hijack — only you passed it on to the Soviets. You used Simpson.'

'He had the MOD Ardarroch schedules; the Kremlin wanted Spearfish: it seemed reasonable to bring them together. Only Simpson didn't know it.'

'And the KGB provided the private navy: Andersen's crowd. Which was why he — Scarred-Hand — didn't try an stop me killing him at the end. He knew failure meant his execution one way or another . . .'

Crofts suddenly stopped, ignoring the Luger. One of the most recent, yet also one of the most inexplicable riddles of all was still unanswered.

'It doesn't even begin to make sense, Harry. You've admitted you're working for the Soviets; you know as well as I do that Spearfish had to be the biggest espionage prize they could ever have hoped for — yet you sabotaged Scarred-Hand's mission, just when he'd virtually pulled it off. You even conned me into helping you.'

Mearns halted then. When Crofts turned cautiously to face him he realised, even through the blackness, that Harry Mearns was grinning again. His features were twisted by what must have been excruciating pain, but he still managed that grin.

'You've heard of double-bluff?'

'Meaning?'

'Remember the research scientist, Thomson?'

'The one murdered in Copenhagen? Eric hinted you knew something about that.'

'The KGB killed the little queer while he was defecting. *Mokri dela* – a "wet job", Crofts: they got a tidy name for everything.'

'What in hell's name for? Working at Ardarroch testing grounds he must have had the Spearfish secrets in his head, Mearns. You don't kill the goose before it's laid the golden egg.'

'Oh, Thomson talked,' Harry assured him blandly. 'Thomson told the Soviet Embassy's technical boys everything before he died.'

'The mutilations – torture?'

'Persuasion,' Harry amended, unabashed. 'Yeah, partly anyway. Seemingly Thomson had a stubborn conviction that knowledge ought to have bought him protection. He wasn't too enthusiastic about divulging the final details of the tactical computer. Maybe he was convinced they'd kill him once he'd spilled everything.'

'It also appeared he was right.'

' 'Course he was.' Harry shrugged reflectively. 'Really, he was a clever little bugger when you think about it.'

'You still haven't explained – the point in eliminating him when he was already a defector. Why not simply smuggle him back to Russia?'

'That's where the bluff came in. If the Brits had thought for a moment that Thomson had spilled the secrets, then they'd have gone straight back to the drawing board; changed the design an' maybe even come up with something more lethal. So the KGB had to camouflage Thomson's death to look as though it had been committed *before* he had time to betray any sensitive information – like, say, the over-enthusiastic work of a homosexual Danish boy friend he'd collected en route. *And* the British fell for it – the

Spearfish programme has been continuing precisely as scheduled.'

'Then why,' Crofts muttered, 'did the Soviets need to mount a second, totally unnecessary attempt tonight? Why risk being caught out when they already have the torpedo's secrets?'

Mearns hesitated. He seemed to be listening for something now. Abruptly he jerked the Luger. 'Get moving; we don't have long. Either of us.'

They climbed further, slipping and sliding and stumbling in the darkness. Every step must have been agony for Mearns; God, but he was a tough campaigner whichever side he was on.

'Why, Mearns? Why did the KGB go after something they'd already got?'

'Because they couldn't afford not to. It's the espionage game, Crofts: I told you – bluff and double bluff. Look, suppose the Brits weren't convinced that Thomson had died without compromising Spearfish . . . say they'd *intentionally* revealed details of that Auxiliary's delivery trip to Ardarroch?'

Crofts thought about Simpson again then, and how competent he'd always seemed. And began to wonder. 'Deliberately fed them to some Soviet mole within MOD Navy, you mean?'

'It was a possibility the Kremlin had to consider. That the British security service were dangling a carefully-prepared carrot.'

'Meaning if they didn't take the bait – at least try for it – then it tended to suggest they'd already got it?'

'Exactly. So the Russians had to be seen to rise to the challenge. They'd no choice: having been presented with Simpson's proposition, they *had* to mount a genuine attempt to hijack that trials weapon.'

Crofts frowned. It still didn't make complete sense. 'Except it could equally have rebounded *against* them had the British taken Thomson's death at face value. The KGB could have queered their own pitch by being too bloody clever: stealing a secret they already had, and so throwing away any gains they'd already made . . .'

'Ah, but they *didn't* manage to, did they?' Harry said. 'Steal it, I mean.'

It was Crofts turn to halt abruptly, forgetfully. Harry raised the gun a fraction but he didn't shoot. He was watching Crofts sardonically.

'You?' Crofts muttered.

'And you. You're far too modest, Major: you did most of the shooting yourself. It's bloody ironic when you think about it – that when you hit the *Marauder* crowd you were, in reality, working for the nastier face of the Politburo. A mission within a mission, Major. Andersen – your Scarred-Hand – was expendable right from the start. You were set-up by sheer chance: he was set-up as an operational necessity. Andersen's KGB orders were to hijack Spearfish, yeah – but mine were the really vital ones . . . to make damn sure he was seen to fail!'

Crofts gazed down the slope at Mearns. Oh, there was real bitterness in him now, and a helplessness of hate. All that killing, all those innocents sacrificed in a giant game of espionage chess. Obliterated simply to give substance to one lie which, in turn, supported yet another lie.

'And incidentally making sure you still came out of it smelling of roses from the British angle, eh, Harry? The sinner repented. The guy who's conscience finally turned against the Russian bear?'

'The only man left alive on that ship, I'd have been the greatest British patriot since Churchill,' Mearns grinned. He was listening again, and abruptly he gestured with the gun. Crofts heard it too, then. The distant drone of an approaching aircraft. The sands of his life-glass were running out fast.

'Your Irish pilot? Harry Mearns' personal get-you-home-to-Mother Russia service now I've screwed it up for you?'

'To the Republic, first. Then the Middle East through IRA gun-running channels. Syria, maybe. Or Libya. The Soviet Embassies look after me from then on.'

'You should feel very much at home with them, Harry,'

Crofts retorted. Harry didn't seem to hear him.

'D'you know, I've never even been to Russia,' Mearns said. But there was no wistful anticipation in the way he said it: more an uncertainty, and a regret for things forever closed to him now.

'You'll get there, Sergeant Major,' Crofts snapped. 'But don't feel too bad about it – we all go to hell in the end. You'll just be goin' while you're still alive.'

They were at the top of the cliff now. The wind was rising to a spiteful moan. Inland Crofts could make out the high, wild horizon which marked the mountains backing Auchenzie village: straight ahead the breaks in the blackness which indicated the old airfield ruins. No investigating headlights: no chance of a last minute reprieve. And then, in the distance, he caught the gleam of a single tiny yellow light – Tarvit farmhouse. Where Laura Harley would still be waiting, enduring her loneliness of bereavement; still not knowing whether Eric's death had finally been avenged; certainly never guessing that Crofts was living the last few seconds of his life within a mile of her bleak vigil.

Harry crested the brow of the path behind him and stopped abruptly. Already Crofts could feel the hairs on the back of his neck cringing; the sweat of anticipation trickling down his brow.

'You aren't going to die unrecognised, you know,' Harry said consolingly. 'They'll make you a hero, Major – even though it is only a Hero of the Supreme Soviet Union.'

Hate was rising in Crofts again. A searing resentful hate, particularly at having been used. 'Explain that, Mearns.'

'When British counter-intellgence find your body they'll prove from forensic tests that you, for whatever crazy reason, fired most of the rounds that aborted Andersen's espionage mission. Right?'

'Go on.'

'It means you've just guaranteed the success of the Soviet plan. You said it yourself just then – I'd have come out of it a British hero: now I'm goin' to leave you with that honour. The Brits will never quite figure why you did it, but sure as hell they won't ever connect *you* with any Kremlin-inspired plot. You've always been one of the good guys at heart, Mickey boy: pure St George an' the dragon underneath that mercenary exterior . . . there never *was* any connection to make. You've really added the icing of conviction to our KGB cake, Major. You began to do that from the moment you first arrived in Auchenzie.'

Crofts snatched a glance over the cliff into Quarry Cove. There were still fires burning aboard the wreck, and the dim white breakers against the shattered pier. But nothing else. It was like staring into the bottomless black pit of Hades.

The aircraft's sound was directly above them now; over-flying; preparing his approach – and Mearns would still have to lay out landing flares; give him a line of the runway. Time was virtually up.

'Who killed Eric Harley?' Crofts almost snarled. 'F'r Christ's sake, Mearns – was Eric working for Simpson or for the Soviets, or even for the British? *Was* he a traitor or not?'

'Sorry, Major,' Harry's voice was uncharacteristically sombre now: almost regretful. 'You've just reached the end of your last campai . . .'

Crofts launched himself crazily off the edge of the black cliff even as the Luger in Harry Mearns hand exploded; scarring his neck with the powder burns, the first shot actually ripping his ear lobe.

Mearns fired again, three more shots in rapid succession, trying to follow him down. But Crofts didn't really care about that by then.

He was falling into nothingness, not even knowing how far his death lay below. Something solid, a branch perhaps, held him briefly, then pitched him on again. Twigs stung his face, checked his fall, but still the fall went on. He heard himself screaming. And then, after an eternity of terror, he hit something slightly softer than a rock, but still harder than any human body could withstand.

And the blackness of the pit closed over and smothered him. And Major Michael Crofts mercifully ceased to feel anything at all.

CHAPTER TWENTY-TWO

The hotel room had been dark and secret for their love-making. And oh, she was so desirable, Pam Trevelyan, with her long blonde curls swirling across the pillow and her exciting impish laugh and her glorious abandonment.

Even as he lay so pleasantly half-waking, half-sleeping on his back Crofts was conscious of his touching her; fondling her. Stroking her glinting stranded pride of hair; her skin so smooth and young; her cheeks, her pert nose, her exquisitely fashioned brows.

Lightly Crofts ran the tip of his finger down, the slightest wisping touch, to follow the high, seductively arrogant plane of her cheekbone, her lower lashes, her closed and sleeping eyelid . . .

. . . her EYELID?

And that was when Crofts jerked erect, staring into the cloying blackness.

Because there wasn't any eyelid there, all of a sudden! Now, quite shockingly, there was nothing . . . except for a ghastly tattered cavity – a wet, oozing, bloodied HOLE where Pamela Trevelyan's blue eye used to be.

Crofts shrieked '*Jesus!*' in a skirl of terror; propelling himself away from the still-warm inhuman thing beside him; scrabbling and retching with revulsion at what was happening to him; twisting frantically yet hardly daring to bring himself to look again upon that recent, awful bed-mate.

Until, slowly, realisation dawned. Oh, it was dark, yes. But not the darkness of the loving bed; it was the chill, sighing darkness of the Scottish night which still clamped over Quarry Cove. And the corpse beside him – the cadaver which must have borne the brunt of Crofts' desperate plunge – was really that of a man.

Wriggling back to the corpse he examined it minutely with the detachment of one who had seen too many corpses – and found himself peering into the barely recognisable features of the second of Harry Mearns' farmer boys.

Meinheer Kruger's – or was it van der Spuy's – right eye had ceased to exist. Whoever had shot him had performed the act cleanly. One round only, immaculately placed. Now only the left orb stared at Crofts in surprised and Cyclopean vacancy, but there was no final glazing yet, death had barely begun its work of dissolution. Crofts laid his hand upon the waxen, destroyed face and felt again the warmth. Whoever had killed the second Boer must have done so very recently.

Only moments before he and Mearns had struggled from the wreck – perhaps even as they were preoccupied with their own desperate fight for survival. Who could possibly have been alive on that beach apart from them? Andersen's men had all died, there had been no survivors. Mearns' third man could have had no reason to do it, surely? In fact Crofts guessed uneasily that somewhere close by in the darkness, Mearns' third man was lying every bit as dead as his colleague – so *who* in God's name was carrying on killing even though the Spearfish nightmare had surely passed its peak?

Grimly, painfully, Crofts dragged himself erect and shook his head. His arm was hanging loose, probably fractured; his own near-corpse was a sea of bruised agony threatening to engulf him yet again. His ear dripped blood in a steady trickle, which was hardly surprising seeing it had recently been shot by a Luger.

How long had passed? How long had he been lying unconscious while Mearns made good his escape?

Then Crofts heard the sound of the aircraft from inland, and listened intently and detected that is was losing, not clawing for height. It was still making its approach *into* Tarvit airstrip against the onshore wind. He stumbled toward the body of the Boer and began to search around in desperation. A gun . . . the man must have carried some kind of gun. He found a torch and flicked it on – it was red; the red of a leading mark, the red of innocent men's blood. Immediately he caught the glint of metal near one outstretched hand and snatched it up.

It was a toy, a mockery of a real soldier's handgun – a .32 ACP Hungarian Frommer with a pathetic seven shot magazine. A bloody useless weapon for shooting at aeroplanes. Jeeze, not even the seagulls of Quarry Cove had cause to fear that.

Crofts began to swear, softly at first but then with growing frustration. And that was a very foolish luxury to allow himself, because Crofts' frustration had already caused the abandonment of his caution once before. Yet caution was the only thing which could keep a far-too-angry man like Crofts alive.

So bloody WHAT!

Carelessly he whirled anyway. And began to drag himself to the top of the cliffs for the second time that night.

It was a nightmare journey for Crofts, accomplished only by the determination of his hate. Stumbling and staggering from the cliff road across the mounds and hummocks of dune; skidding in liquid sand which avalanched from under his heels as he clawed his way to the top of every obstacle; the gorse whipping his face; the long sea-grass clutching devil's tentacles around his ankles at every rasping step . . . and it was all for nothing even when he got there. It had all been f'r bloody nothing!

He knew he was far too late when he first raised mad-wild eyes above the level of the last low crest and the airstrip stretched before him. Already the aircraft had taxied back inland and was turning to begin its take-off out to sea.

There were flare-pots hissing at both ends of the cracked runway – laying out and igniting them must have been a massive effort for Mearns with his savaged shoulder. But they gave enough light for Crofts to detect Harry in the distance, a tiny, almost pathetic figure; struggling against the slipstream; attempting to clamber through the cockpit door of the twin-engined aircraft even as it pivoted on one wheel, glass-clear propeller discs mirroring the glare of the chemical markers.

It was a blue and white 310 Cessna with long rapier nose and rakish style, and the registration letters whitewashed over to avoid identification. Even as Crofts began to run heedlessly along the open runway the matchstick figure of Harry Mearns finally clambered inside and the door slammed shut. Then the aircraft and Crofts were alone – each facing the other: a buzzing Goliath against a touchingly inadequate David.

Immediately the note of the Cessna's twin engines began to rise, surging in a roar of power, whirling and shredding the smoke from the flare pots in great streamers astern. Crofts could see the ailerons moving; the elevator testing as the giant wasp trembled on the threshold of take-off . . . and then, slowly at first but with ever-increasing speed it began to surge towards him.

Crofts still kept on running down the runway. Crofts, and Harry Mearns' aeroplane, were shortly about to meet.

Crofts *was* insane then; just for those few brief seconds as he and the circular-saw disc of that starboard aircraft propeller narrowed the gap between them. Crofts had accepted that there was no way he could prevent Mearns from leaving Scotland by shooting at him with a toy gun – though he still did, mind you; seven pathetic times as he ran towards the Cessna. Christ, he even threw the gun at it after that . . . but it was a silly, useless gesture; executed much too soon and only emphasising his own lack of balance.

There was only one other way. He just kept on running, tortured lungs a maniac bellow, straight for the propeller of that onrushing plane.

At take-off speed it couldn't take *that* much to throw a light aircraft into an uncontrollable, fatal skid. Surely not more than the impact of striking . . . say . . . a human body?

It was curious, the way it happened in the end.

It was only a fleeting shadow; hardly enough to register in

Crofts' temporarily short-circuited brain. Just the merest suggestion of something passing ponderously across the runway; momentarily breaking the line of sight between Crofts and those roaring incoming discs.

Something squarish – remotely familiar. Emitting a chugging resonance at odds with the full-power snarl of an aircraft engine. Then it had passed between them and there was only the speeding aircraft, and Crofts' berserk shriek of fury. And maybe five seconds more of the ultimate terror even the bravest of men must feel.

And that was the moment when the curious happening . . . well . . . happened.

Because without any warning, there came the most fiendish screech of exploding metal ever heard – a monstrous cacophony of destruction; a buzz-saw of disintegration echoing across the silent dunes towards Auchenzie; screeling and squealing and twanging and rending.

Whereupon the whole 310 Cessna with the blue and white livery and the painted-out registration suddenly flipped up its tail and stood on its nose, and dug its port wingtip into the runway at maybe seventy knots.

And began to cartwheel towards Crofts, even as the high octane fuel in its rupturing wing tanks detonated in a first flash of rapidly expanding fire.

When Crofts registered that barely credible scene he became sane in the blink of a thunderstruck eye.

Bawling a shocked, 'Jesus CHRIST!' he jinked violently to his left, still running flat out. Then, as the cartwheeling Cessna got bigger and bigger, he finally flung himself full length along the runway – to find himself staring into the contorted, soundlessly-shrieking features of Harry Mearns!

But Harry was only passing by – upside down at that, in the brief image of their final meeting: still strapped securely within the perspex cockpit and with the flames already reaching up and licking him in white-hot anticipation of what they would do to him. And then Harry was gone without even the courtesy of recognition as the crumpled wing tip carved its way a hand's breadth above Crofts to leave him watching Harry's skipping coffin blow up in an expanding, runaway ball of molten alloy.

He staggered to his feet eventually, after the last explosion had died along with Company Sergeant Major Mearns, late of mercenary Column Delta – and the *Komitet Gosudarstevennoy Bezopasnosti*.

It didn't take him as long, this time, to solve the latest riddle of the Spearfish affair.

Harry's aircraft had crashed because it hadn't been given much alternative – it had run at full take-off power into a wire rope stretched across the runway!

By the light of the flames, Crofts quickly found one end of the rope – which did look remarkably like a certain recently-discarded hand crane lifting wire, by the way. It was attached, roughly at light aircraft propeller height, to the framework of the old control tower itself.

It took a few more moments of reeling and following and stumbling blindly over parts of eviscerated 310 Cessna to discover where the other end of the rope was attached. And, coincidentally, the means by which it had been so efficiently dragged across the runway at precisely the critical time.

To a battered Land Rover with a missing windscreen. To Eric Harley's old Land Rover, in fact; now standing silent and untended beside Den of Tarvit airfield.

Crofts was already whirling, feeling the sick frustration back in his belly again and wishing to God he hadn't used all the rounds in that bloody useless Boer's weapon, when he heard the snick of a submachine gun being set to 'Fire'.

Followed by an urbane, really quite conversational voice.

'It never seems to end, does it, old boy? All the unpleasantness and the aggravation. The sheer futility of people's insistence on dying, even for the most unworthy of causes.'

'Hello, Simpson,' Crofts said.

Resignedly.

CHAPTER TWENTY-THREE

Even Commander Edward Simpson, RN, looked rumpled this time, and somewhat damp. But Simpson was a proper shipwrecked sailor, not a wet soldier posing as one like Crofts, so it was perfectly understandable.

Crofts noticed the blood congealing in Simpson's hair. Mearns' hurried snap-shot had obviously been a painful experience, but it only went to underline what a tough bird Simpson really was.

Like, say, a sea eagle. With a machinegun.

'You killed the Boer down on the beach, Simpson?'

'Both of them, old son. Surprisingly decent chaps in many ways. They made the mistake of helping me scramble ashore. A charitable act.'

'And Mulders? Did you kill him too?'

'An over-garrulous man, and one can't afford talkative men in our profession. I'd had you under surveillance all night. It was hard not to intervene while your police escorts were being . . . ah, disposed of.'

Crofts turned and stared dully down the airstrip. The flames were dying now, like all the people concerned with Spearfish seemed to be. Soon somebody had to come . . . it was only a question of whether he would still be around to greet them. He began to get angry with himself for wasting what little time he might have left.

'You were working for British counter-intelligence all the time, weren't you, Simpson? That hijack and blackmail cover of yours were just bait for the Soviets; to establish whether they *had* already gained the Spearfish secrets from the defector, Thomson.'

Simpson bowed mockingly. 'They swallowed it, too. They'll believe their bluff worked – that we're complacent now – but we're already redesigning the tactical computer to counter any gains they've made. It'll add a year to the development programme: a small enough price for Thomson's treason; and they'll never try for it again after this.'

'Eric Harley, Simpson. *Did* you kill him?'

The colourless eyes glittered in the fading light of Mearns' cremation. 'Sadly – yes.'

It didn't come as a shock. Not now. Crofts was already drained of feeling: there only remained that awful sadness over all the things the four of them – he, Laura, Eric . . . and Pam Trevelyan – might have been able to do together if Spearfish had never happened.

'Sadly?' he jeered. There was only spitefulness left. Not that he could hurt Simpson's feelings. Simpson was a monster. Nothing could hurt Commander bloody Simpson, Royal Navy not-at-all retired except, maybe, a stake through the heart at sunrise.

'With the *deepest* regret, old boy,' Simpson replied sharply, and with unexpected pique. 'I never enjoy terminating a member of my own side, Crofts. Especially a particularly brave one.'

Crofts face was expressionless now. Even the spite had drained away. 'His mistake was in *being* a patriot: in blowing the whistle on the Soviets, wasn't it? When he discovered Mearns and Scarred-Hand were more than just criminal mercenaries – really were Russian agents – he came to Naval Security without realising it was a British set-up from the start: that you'd *challenged* them to try for Spearfish. And that made him a threat to you as well.'

'We had to ensure he wouldn't give our counter-bluff away under pressure. He was cracking up, Crofts; Mearns or Andersen would have noticed eventually, and made him talk.'

Crofts didn't really need to try the last piece into the Auchenzie jigsaw, he already knew it would fit. But he wanted to finish his self-imposed task neatly before he died.

'You deliberately set me up as prime suspect for Eric's murder, didn't you? You salvaged my Beretta, then pretended to bump into me in London in order to entice me to Den of Tarvit. My old affair with Laura allowed you to devise a motive for Harley's death that wouldn't scare the Soviets off.'

'Your Scarred-Hand worked on much the same principle when he killed your police escorts, old boy. He needed to ensure you stayed on the run to prevent Constable Plod's deeper interest in associated mayhem on the farm,' Simpson pointed out reasonably. 'We're all the same in the end, don't you see? It's a bloody business, this Cold War.'

Crofts gazed at Commander Simpson RN through the grey dawn light. Simpson was smiling at him. It was the same smile Mearns had shown when he'd told Crofts how clever and how ruthless *his* side had been. The Machiavellian face of the espionage game.

'There is supposed to be a difference, Simpson,' he said bitterly. 'But somehow I don't think you'd understand, even if I explained it. D'you know something?'

'Tell me, old son.'

'I'm glad I screwed your plan up tonight. It's the only goddam good thing that's happened to me since I came up here – that I didn't help either of you; either you Brits or the bloody Russians. Compared to you, being a mercenary soldier is an honest living. I hope everyone of you espionage bastards – British, Russian, French, American, Bulgarian – I hope you all roast in hell for what you're doing to the world.'

Simpson stretched and gazed over to where the wreck of the Cessna burned out at the end of the runway, and further on to where the last smoke from *Marauder* twisted lazily into the now clear sky.

'Some of us already are in hell, Major – oh, and by the way . . .'

'What?'

'Don't feel too virtuous. You did help us you know; all of us. You helped the Soviets because they got, or thought they got, exactly what they wanted – an aborted attempt made even more realistic than they could have prayed for. Some crazy guy called Crofts thwarted it in the end, and left absolutely no reason for our Intelligence people to make any connection with Moscow. And what they don't realise yet won't harm them. Until the next Battle of the Atlantic starts.'

Crofts would have liked to kill Simpson then, but he knew he couldn't. No way. Not there, in the condition he was in. 'And you – the British?'

Simpson smiled again. A slow, mocking smile. The sort that Scarred-Hand used to smile when he was being particularly sadistic.

'You're still helping, Crofts. Just by staying alive. At first you didn't matter; you were simply my front for killing Harley. Only you got over-zealous, more deeply involved than I ever thought you would . . . until now you're an even more convincing scapegoat, the icing on our cake. Your existence will do more than anything else to prove to the Soviets that there *was* no British security counter-plot. Ostensibly they were foiled by one resolute, bloody-minded, thoroughly Anglo-Saxon hero and no other agency.'

Harry Mearns had said much the same thing. In practically the same words. Only he'd been revelling in it from the KGB's point of view.

Crofts shook his bloodied, aching head as Simpson laid the unnecessary machinegun down at last; a casual reprieve. He was still a loser, anyway. Every way he turned he was a loser while Simpson had won every ace in the pack. Or was he? Simpson still seemed a bit regretful as he gazed over towards the silent Land Rover and the wire which had cartwheeled Mearns' aeroplane into a ball of fire.

'Pity you set that up, old boy. I'd have enjoyed a chat with our mutual friend Harry, before closing the books.'

Crofts frowned uncertainly. 'Set what up?'

'Your tripwire execution. Clever stuff, Crofts: Christ only knows how you managed it in the time . . .'

'Simpson!' Crofts snapped urgently.

'Mmmm?'

'I didn't set it up at all, Simpson. I'd automatically assumed that *you* did . . .'

And that was when he heard a crack behind him; noticed from the corner of his eye that a clump of gorse had moved. Someone was *hiding* in there.'

Ohhh, Jesus, not *again*!

He was swinging with jangling, already impossibly-stretched nerves even before he recognised who it was. And then he halted abruptly and felt sick and sad, and sympathetic.

Laura Harley stood there. Looking at them. There were fresh tears in her eyes and she looked so remote; so hopelessly lost.

Crofts sensed instantly that she must have heard everything. Including the callous, so very trivial reasons for her husband's execution.

CHAPTER TWENTY-FOUR

There was something about her. Something unsettling . . .

Crofts couldn't place it. All he knew was that it frightened him a great deal. It seemed to worry Simpson, too. Even Commander Simpson, Royal Navy, looked uneasy for the first time since Crofts had known him.

'You heard then, Mrs Harley?' he probed uncertainly.

Crofts said, 'Laura? God, I'm sorry you had to learn this way, Laura.'

She looked at him then and he could see his sympathy for her mirrored in her concern for him. She said calmly, 'It's all right, Mike. Really it is.'

She turned to face Simpson. 'I heard, Commander. And I understood. Perfectly.'

Crofts stared at her. She *understood*? Already he could see Simpson relaxing imperceptibly and hated him even more for it. The naval officer stepped forward and gave a self-conscious bow.

'Please, Mrs Harley, may I offer my condolences. His death was regrettable, but you must still believe your husband died a patriot.'

Crofts found his voice; gesturing towards the Land Rover and the lethal tripwire. 'You did that, Laura? All by yourself.'

She seemed vague, lost. 'I . . . didn't know what else to do. I felt so helpless. But I'd seen the wire when we were here together, and I knew *someone* evil might try to fly away.'

She was still frowning; looking at them. Crofts frowned too and followed her gaze but there was nothing; only Scotland, with the barren mountains and the gently waving dune-grass and the morning song of birds and the blue-cold sky. And then he understood that was why she had been hesitating – because there *was* nothing else. No exceptional movement.

'Why, Commander? The plane crash, the explosions . . . but not a soul has arrived. Not even the local police.'

Simpson smiled reassuringly. 'Oh, they're all there, Mrs Harley. Around your boundaries. This was declared a secure area immediately we knew *Marauder* was heading in.'

'But I'm here,' Laura pointed out reasonably.

'You were already inside the net. I'd overlooked you.'

Crofts couldn't stand the small talk any longer. It was all as irrelevant as . . . Eric's death. He swung away and felt dizzy.

'Sick bay, old boy?' Simpson asked cheerfully, though God knew he looked as though he needed to go himself. Laura frowned.

'What about Michael, Commander? Surely he's cleared of suspicion now . . . or can he ever be? Isn't all this secret?'

'Free as a bird, Mrs Harley. It's where secrets can help. The authorities – police, judiciary, even the press – have already been advised that what we've known as the Spearfish affair was merely a rogue terrorist group attempting to embarrass Her Majesty's Government.' Simpson turned to grin patronisingly, rather slyly at Crofts. 'You're news, Major. As far as the world is concerned you're a thoroughly decent hero-figure battered by the caprices of fate. And that's official!'

Laura was close to them now and suddenly Crofts was frowning. There *was* something wrong: something out of place. She was wearing a neat enough coat, yet it hung badly somehow. Dragged down to one side.

'But surely others must know the truth, Commander. Some of your own security people must be aware of his real part in the Spearfish affair.'

'Not at the moment. Not until I've made out my report . . .'

Crofts began to shout, 'No! F'r God's sake, Laura – NO!'

'I'm very glad of that, Commander,' Laura whispered.

And then she shot Simpson four times. Quite coldly. Right in the pit of the stomach.

With the Beretta Model M951 which Crofts had recognised the instant she dragged it from her pocket.

There had only been four rounds left in the magazine when he'd given it to her earlier. The final three were totally unnecessary.

She didn't really care after that, but Crofts did it all the same. For her.

He gently took Beretta M951 from her hand after she'd cried the last of her tears, and walked over to where the remains of Harry Mearns' burned-out aircraft were smeared across the runway. There were two charred, monkey-sized dolls still smoking and melting where the cockpit had been. Without compassion, Crofts threw the Beretta into the wreckage between them and went back to put his arms around Laura.

They would never quite know how Mearns had managed to kill brave Commander Simpson before he took off, but it wouldn't matter. There were already too many questions requiring answers from too many people now dead. Laura would be perfectly safe.

And Simpson *did* have to die, you know. Oh, not simply because of Eric Harley and the two policemen and the expendable men of the Auxiliary. Not only for them, and for the peace of mind of Crofts.

Laura had killed him because she knew that, while Simpson was alive and free to plot and counter-plot and terminate people under a cloak of official secrecy, neither she nor Crofts would ever be safe. That somewhere, somehow, some quiet day long after other people had forgotten the 'terrorist' incident, there would still occur a nasty accident.

For wouldn't it have been expedient, and typical of Simpson's cold war philosophy – that he should make absolutely certain, once and for all, that no one ever could relate the real truth: the way the pieces really had fitted together, in the Spearfish jigsaw puzzle?

EPILOGUE

Crofts telephoned Pamela Trevelyan that same evening.

He rang her from the tattered callbox in the little high street of Auchenzie. Laura Harley sat outside in the ikon gold Mercedes while he did so. He gazed with renewed affection at his pride through the grimy windows while he waited for his connection; the Strathclyde Police had cared for it well. You would never have imagined, looking at it, that it had once been under arrest.

Awkwardly lighting a Lucky Strike he eased his tightly bandaged arm. The scrawled legends captured his momentary attention; still assuring him that *Eck* did love *Jessie*, and that the *Govan Huns wis OK*. He was happy for the Govan Huns, but a little uncertain about Eck and Jessie. Had Eck written that in a euphoric moment after he'd first met Jessie? Had she loved Eck just as much, or was that merely a delusion on Eck's part? Come to that, were *his* feelings for Pamela Trevelyan only a reflection of his foolishness?

And them Pam's voice; so excited and loving all at the same time. Until she started to cry with the sheer happiness of it, and Crofts knew he hadn't been foolish at all.

'The hotel where we met,' he ordered eventually. 'I'll drive down and meet you there tomorrow evening. Can you book a room?'

Pam giggled all the way from London, and said, 'Only until we can buy a flat . . .' and then she added a funny 'Oh!', and Crofts asked anxiously, 'What?'

'Daddy told me everything in confidence that you wanted to know about, well, the "Thinking Thing". That swims underwater. Do you still need the information now?'

He thought a long time before he answered. He didn't want to lie to her, but it had been savage stuff . . . unpleasant. She was very young, innocent; she could never have believed it anyway.

Well, when you think about it, not even he had really been able to, had he? Or not for a long time.

'No,' he said. 'They were only vicious hoodlums. It wasn't anything to do with spies after all.'

He met the Ferocious Mother just as he stepped from the box. Crofts half-stepped back in terror as she shuddered to a halt with the pram and gazed at him with a fearsome glint.

'You'll be away back tae London now?' she interrogated him sharply.

'Tomorrow morning,' he hastened to assure her. 'Very early.'

'Aye?'

She stared at him, tight-lipped as a zipped-up purse, then snapped, 'Just as well! It's people like you fae outside cause all the bother here. This wis a quiet wee village 'til you came wi' your shiny motor car. Ah'm thinking you must hae been responsible for it all yourself.'

'Well, not *quite*.'

'It's no' a secret, ye ken. Oh, mebbe you think it is – but it's no'!'

He stared at her blankly, disbelievingly; almost cowering back into the phone booth until she abruptly dismissed him by steering her baby tank away with head in air. But how did she know – how much could she know?

She'd gone barely ten yards when she turned again to fire her last broadside.

'Och, it's an absolute and utter disgrace – an educated man like yourself. Doing all yon vandalism to a public telephone box!'

Crofts was grinning as he finally returned to Laura and the Mercedes. The sadly too recent widow smiled bravely back with only the tiniest hint of drying tears.

Eric would always be there between them: they both accepted that. Which was why, tomorrow, Crofts would take her to London where Eric's body was already waiting, and husband and wife together would fly back to Eric's beloved Africa where they would stay, and where Crofts would probably never meet either of them again.

But Crofts and Laura Harley would still mean something deep and very dear to each other, even then. Because the two of them shared another secret now.

And a secret – between friends, anyway – is a truly priceless bond.